Focus Groups

Focus Groups: From structured interviews to collective conversations is a conceptual and practical introduction to focus groups. As the title indicates, focus groups traditionally encompass a wide range of discursive practices. These span from formal structured interviews with particular people assembled around clearly delimited topics to less formal, open-ended conversations with large and small groups that can unfold in myriad and unpredictable ways. Additionally, focus groups can and have served many overlapping purposes—from the pedagogical, to the political, to the traditionally empirical. In this book, focus groups are systematically explored; not as an extension or elaboration of interview work alone, but as its own specific research method with its own particular affordances.

This book comprehensively explores:

- *the nature of focus groups*
- *political and activist uses of focus groups*
- *practical ways to run a successful focus group*
- *effective analysis of focus group data*
- *contemporary threats to focus groups.*

Focus Groups: From structured interviews to collective conversations is essential reading for qualitative researchers at every level, particularly those involved in education, nursing, social work, anthropology, and sociology disciplines.

George Kamberelis is a Wyoming Excellence Chair of Literacy Education at the University of Wyoming.

Greg Dimitriadis is Professor of Educational Leadership and Policy at the Graduate School of Education, University of Buffalo, The State University of New York.

Focus Groups

From structured interviews to collective conversations

George Kamberelis and Greg Dimitriadis

Routledge
Taylor & Francis Group

LONDON AND NEW YORK

First published 2013
by Routledge
2 Park Square, Milton Park, Abingdon, Oxon OX14 4RN

Simultaneously published in the USA and Canada
by Routledge
711 Third Avenue, New York, NY 10017

Routledge is an imprint of the Taylor & Francis Group, an informa business

British Library Cataloguing in Publication Data
A catalogue record for this book is available from the British Library

Library of Congress Cataloging in Publication Data
Kamberelis, George.
  Focus groups : from structured interviews to collective conversations /
George Kamberelis and Greg Dimitriadis.
    p. cm.
  1. Focus groups. I. Dimitriadis, Greg, 1969– II. Title.
  H61.28.K36 2013
  001.4′33—dc23   2012034009

ISBN: 978–0–415–69226–7 (hbk)
ISBN: 978–0–415–69227–4 (pbk)
ISBN: 978–0–203–59044–7 (ebk)

Typeset in Galliard
by Swales & Willis Ltd, Exeter, Devon

Printed and bound in Great Britain by
TJ International Ltd, Padstow, Cornwall

Contents

Acknowledgments

We would like to thank Norman Denzin and Yvonna Lincoln for their original invitation to write about focus groups for the third and fourth editions of *The Handbook of Qualitative Research* (Sage, 2005, 2011). This book builds upon and extends many of the ideas and arguments presented in those chapters. We would also like to thank Norman for inviting us to conduct workshops on focus groups for his annual Congress of Qualitative Inquiry. During those workshops, our interactions with scholars from around the world contributed in important ways to our ongoing thinking about focus groups and focus group research. Thanks also go out to Katherine Ryan for first suggesting we turn our ideas about focus groups into a book, and for the many pithy ideas she has shared with us since then. Finally, we would like to thank Philip Mudd at Routledge for supporting this project from its inception to its completion.

Chapter 1

Focus groups

A brief and incomplete history

Focus groups have become a part of the collective consciousness of the qualitative research community and of the public imagination. Recall here the extensive use of focus groups on virtually all the major US networks following the US presidential and vice-presidential debates of 2008. Although these were sometimes called "polls," or "town hall meetings," they all exhibited the forms and functions of large-scale focus groups as most people understand them. The first debate in Columbus, Ohio, was particularly instructive. The CNN press release noted:

> Special correspondent Soledad O'Brian will moderate a focus group in Columbus, Ohio. The group will be comprised of a selection of voters from the hotly contested state. During the debate, the participants will operate electronic dial testers that will allow television viewers to see the group's reaction in real time.
>
> (CNN, 2008)

This group was made up of voters who had not yet decided about their vote. Their individual reactions, as noted, were measured in "real time" by way of a special meter that registered positive, negative, or indifferent responses. Afterwards, they were gathered together and queried about their responses.

SOLEDAD O'BRIAN: Barbara, you are 71 years old. Hold the mike up pretty close so we can get to hear you pretty well. I was watching you watch the debate. It was so interesting because you had a rapt attention and you were working your little dial like crazy, what resonated with you?

BARBARA HOOPER: Well it was what didn't, if I could speak about that.

O'BRIAN: OK.

HOOPER: I mean, we have so many things going on in our country today, everyone has named so many of those tonight. But I would like for them to have been more specific about the war and a plan on when to bring our troops home. That concerned me a great deal.

(CNN Transcripts, 2008)

Individual group members spoke about their reactions to these debates first and foremost—as Hooper did here. There was very little dialogue between participants and moderator or between and among participants. Moderators like O'Brian tended to be quite directive in their questioning. The goal of the whole enterprise was to elicit a quick snapshot of how messages were taken up (or not) by people across the political spectrum. The end goal was clear—determining whether the debates swayed these undecided voters. Much like the earliest focus group work on propaganda messages in the 1940s, quantitative data (i.e. meters that register a continuum of responses) were privileged but complemented by delimited qualitative data (i.e. participants' interview responses). This pattern is exemplary of the dominant approach to focus group work—an approach that treats focus groups as extensions of one-on-one interviews and subordinates them to what many researchers deem to be "hard" data.

This example highlights the appeal focus groups have had over time, as well as their place in the popular imagination. Both privately and publicly, focus groups are now routinely used to gauge popular attitudes and dispositions. They are used by politicians to test their platforms or to gauge popular sentiment around key issues. They are used by executives in the entertainment industry to test their latest creations—films, television shows, CDs. They are used by marketing analysts in industry to test their latest consumer goods. Indeed, in the media we often see focus groups on spectacular display, taking them out of clandestine offices and putting them in front of a global audience. Looking across these displays, it is remarkable to see how little has changed in use and function of focus groups during the past 70 or more years.

In many respects, CNN's version of focus groups—a part of what the network called the most technologically advanced coverage of any election to date—was old-fashioned. More specifically, the double elision alluded to above has continued to mark much of the work on focus groups to date, particularly in more applied fields. First, focus groups are often not framed as distinct from one-on-one interviews. Instead, they are conceptualized as large interviews. In this regard, we will note much slippage between individual and group data gathering strategies throughout this book. Researchers are still puzzling through the similarities and differences between and among such strategies. Second, data from focus groups are often seen to serve a secondary function in research—to complement quantifiable data gathered using surveys or other instruments. Importantly, both of these elisions can be traced to the earliest use of focus groups in research. And both are still prevalent in contemporary research across a wide range of fields today. Indeed, both were prominent in CNN's coverage of the 2008 elections.

The applied nature of much focus group work helps account for the persistence of this double elision. That is, focus groups have been used to solve a wide array of "real world" or practical problems. Because of their prevalence as practical tools in applied domains, focus groups have been under-theorized. And because they do not rest on a firm conceptual foundation, they are typically reinvented (almost from "scratch") by each new generation of researchers or in relation to new empirical problems.

The origins of focus group research

The use of focus group research extends back to early propaganda or media effects studies at the Bureau of Applied Social Research at Columbia University in the 1940s. Originally founded to study the (then) new media of radio, research was soon undertaken on a wide range of media and their effects. Of particular interest in the post-World War II era was the study of mass-mediated "propaganda." Several new methods emerged from the Bureau including the focus group or "focussed interview." Merton and Kendall (1946) were rather inconsistent in their spelling of focused/focussed. We have chosen to use the more common spelling—focused—throughout. The so-called "focused interview" had the virtue of expediency. It was a way to get relevant, specific information from relatively large numbers of subjects quickly. This approach to focus groups was rooted in positivist or post-positivist epistemologies, which assume that the Truth is "out there" to be efficiently excavated, reported, and used. In many respects, the empirical material that emerged from these early focus groups could be analyzed with the same tools used to analyze one-on-one interviews. Here, focus groups were simply extensions of interviews meant to elicit individual opinions. While taking place in a group, the "unit of analysis" was still the individual.

This look at the beginnings of focus group research highlights the role and importance of "epistemology" in research methodology. As we have argued elsewhere, epistemologies are basic ways of seeing and understanding the world. For example, constructivists understand the world as constituted through human interactions. And thus see "fact" and "value" as interrelated. Positivists and post-positivists understand the world as independent from human interactions and thus see "fact" as completely separate from "value." Epistemologies are different from "theories" which tend to be coherent but also contingent and emergent architectures of ideas. For example, Marxists see oppressive class relations as constitutive of much of how social relations between and among people have been organized throughout human history. Feminists see gender as central. Both epistemologies and theories are distinct from approaches to research and data collection strategies—the frameworks and tools used to gather, interpret, and disseminate empirical findings. See Kamberelis and Dimitriadis (2005) for a fuller explanation of the relations between and among epistemologies, theories approaches, and strategies.

These levels of analyses often get confused and muddled. In particular, researchers and others have tended to conflate positivist epistemologies with quantitative research approaches and strategies, and constructivist epistemologies with qualitative ones. Yet the "paradigm wars" of the 1980s and 1990s, played out in the journal *Educational Researcher* and elsewhere, demonstrated in no uncertain terms that these distinctions do not hold. Much early focus group research was grounded in positivist epistemologies. The Truth was assumed to be out there to be collected through rigorous and highly "focused" interviews—where situations or problems were defined, hypotheses formulated, interview protocol generated, and individuals questioned. Moreover, because the individual was the basic unit of analysis, in this research, the Truth was thought to be located in individual minds. This is not at all surprising given that western science is both a product of the Enlightenment and is still heavily imbued with Enlightenment principles such as Descartes' separation of mind and body and privileging of mind and Leibniz's monadology, where all individuals are unique substances that harbor their unique truths within themselves.

This focus on the individual had disciplinary implications as well. Specifically, by locating the Truth in the individual, focus group research tended to favor psychological approaches and explanations over sociological ones. Indeed, psychological approaches and explanations are dominant within many fields to this day (e.g. education, nursing, and marketing). In contrast (and despite the fact that most major advances in intellectual history during the past few decades have come from social and sociological theory), sociological approaches and explanations have remained marginal in these and other fields. Problems and explanations, here, tend not to be viewed in terms of social forces and structures such as class structure or gender inequalities or race and racism but in the motivations, attitudes, and beliefs of individuals. By thinking of focus groups as extensions of one-on-one interviews key directions for theory and research have been systematically underutilized.

With an eye toward broadening our understanding of the nature and functions of focus groups in research, knowledge generation, and application, *Focus Groups: From Structured Interviews to Collective Conversations* is both a conceptual and a practical introduction to focus group research. As the title indicates, focus groups can and have encompassed a wide range of discursive practices—from formal structured interviews with particular people assembled around clearly delimited topics to less formal, more open-ended conversations with large and small groups that can unfold in myriad and unpredictable ways. In addition, focus groups can serve (and have served) many overlapping purposes—from the pedagogical, to the political, to the traditionally empirical. In this volume, we look to explore focus groups systematically, not as an extension or elaboration of interview work alone, but as its own specific research strategy with its own particular affordances.

This is a practical distinction. The techniques and tools one uses to collect one-on-one interview data cannot easily be imported into focus group settings. Or rather, if they are imported into these settings, they do not usually mine the unique and rich potentials for knowledge generation, pedagogy, and political work that focus groups can afford. But the differences between individual interviews and focus group conversations extend beyond technique alone. There are important theoretical or conceptual distinctions between the two. One-on-one interviews are often undergirded by an Enlightenment notion of the "self." Recall that the Enlightenment was the source of positivist and post-positivist epistemologies. From this perspective, the self is a transcendent consciousness that functions unencumbered by social and material conditions, and that is the source of all knowledge and the agent of all action. Such a self is unified, coherent, autonomous, and non-contradictory. Moreover, the self is radically separate from the external world (the subject–object dichotomy of western thought) and thus able to know this world "objectively" through the rational and/or technical-instrumental separation of subject and object. This separation is achieved in one of two ways. For rationalists or pure theorists, it is achieved through the systematic application of reason to achieve unmediated access to formal principles or the formal logic that makes possible the observables of the world. For empiricists, it is achieved through controlled observation and experimentation with the goal of "finding" interpretation-free brute facts.

In contrast, from a more sociological or social constructionist perspective, the self is seen as produced in and through historical, social, and material practices. Recent post-structuralist accounts of the self are instructive here, especially accounts generated from within critical social theory and cultural studies (e.g. Bourdieu, 1990; deCerteau, 1984; Smith, 1988). In these accounts, the dualism that has thwarted advancement in conceiving the self in relation to social, cultural, and ideological discourses and practices has been rejected and alternatives have been proposed. Selves are seen as simultaneously continuous and contradictory, constituting and constitutive, produced and resistant, and they are animated by two basic and co-implicated processes: the interpellation of individuals into materially, socially, and ideologically formed subject positions, and the negativity or contradiction of being multiply positioned, which spawns resistance to such positioning. This pragmatic yet paradoxical articulation of subjectivity as a process that is both singular and multiple and that is able therefore both to resist discursive and material oppression and to take responsibility for its history is something that most systematic accounts of the self (e.g. Cartesian, utopian Marxist, deconstructionist) have failed to produce. And central to all aspects of this double articulation of subjectivity is the idea that both the interpellation of individuals into multiple subject positions and the negativity inherent in this process that engenders resistance are grounded in the same complex discursive processes. The self, therefore, does not get reduced to an a priori mind, a social formation, or a sign. No particular self can ever be known or guaranteed in advance. Rather, the self is a particular configuration of discursive and material practices that is constantly working on itself—constructing, deconstructing, and reconstructing itself in and by multiple discourses and social practices, their effects, and the ways they intersect, transverse, and challenge one another. Finally, conceived in this way, the "self" is always already the social.

Madriz's (1997) study of women's fear of crime (discussed in more detail in Chapter 2) is an excellent example of how this way of thinking about the relations between the self and the social can play out in focus group work. Through focus group conversations, Madriz realized that fear is, by and large, a collective phenomenon. Although she did not use the same language we are using here to talk about the individual, the collective, and the relations between them, she clearly treated the "group" as the unit of analysis and saw the self and the social as constituting each other. This allowed her to understand fear as a collective phenomenon—not as an atomistic affective entity residing in the minds and bodies of individuals. The implications of her insights in this regard are profound. Fear is to be understood and addressed as a social issue and not a psychological one. To put it perhaps too reductively, a "sociology of fear" supplants the all-too-often evoked "psychology of fear." The "reality" of fear is thus challenged as a normative concept. Once challenged, fear can be imagined, lived, and responded to differently, and we would argue, more productively. The reason for this is that research and its application can now be directed toward the conditions of possibility of women's fears about crime such as institutional sexism.

Focus groups are perfect sites for empirical investigations of these new theoretical formulations of self. In particular, they give us opportunities to see whether and how "self," "other," and "context" seem to be co-emergent phenomena, getting us to the very heart of the social processes social theorists argue constitute reality or the world we live in. In other words, exploring the relations among "self," "other," and "context" can help us answer Foucault's most fundamental question: why is reality organized as it is and not some other way? Again, focus groups are especially fertile sites for such forms of inquiry. But only if we treat focus groups as their own unique method—not as a simple extension of traditional one-on-one interviews, and not as a mere "add on" to quantitative studies. Our approach to focus groups does have this emergent and ecumenical character. As such, it has particular consequences for how we think through the kinds of data we gather in focus group research and what we do with these data.

In this book, we try to develop a workable set of theoretical and practical distinctions that mark focus group work as quasi-unique in the world of method. Although the term "focus group," coined in the middle of the twentieth century by Robert Merton and colleagues in their work on propaganda effects, had very specific meaning as we noted above, we are using the term to cover a much broader range of facilitated social activity. As we have noted, focus groups can be group interviews or collective conversations. Most fall somewhere along the continuum between them. Key here is the degree to which groups are "managed" by the researcher or allowed to develop in more free-flowing and self-organizing ways. When they are allowed to be more free flowing, focus groups can mitigate or inhibit the authority of the researcher, allowing participants to "take over" or "own" the interview space. This allows researchers to explore group dynamics, the lifeblood of social activity, as well as to explore the constitutive power of discourse in people's lives. While not a "natural" occurrence, focus groups allow researchers to create very good approximations to natural interactions than do individual interviews and sometime even observations where the presence of the researcher makes people cautious. Finally, focus groups can allow for what we call "memory synergy" and "political synergy" among participants. These (and other) knowledge generating affordances are in many ways unique to focus group work; they are extraordinarily important for gaining access to and for saturating one's understanding of certain kinds of social phenomena; and we will discuss them in considerable detail in Chapter 3.

We turn now to the earliest work on focus groups, teasing out some key continuities and discontinuities that still pepper the landscape of qualitative inquiry today.

The focus

The researcher puts the "focus" in "focus groups." That is, the researcher typically positions the topic under question a priori. Of course, this can imply a range of directed and less directed approaches. Thus, focus groups can share much with traditional one-on-one interviews. In their most controlled form, individual interviews often imply a dyadic and even clinical relationship between interviewer and interviewee. In this form, the interviewer holds most of the power and authority, extracting information from the interviewee. The control is in the hands of the researcher, who sets the parameters, defines the interview protocol, and channels the flow of discussion. In their less controlled form, the interviewer negotiates an emergent relationship with the interviewee. Control is negotiated, interview protocols are more open-ended, the interviewee is encouraged to introduce topics and manage the "floor," and the conversation is allowed to move in various, even unpredictable, directions.

So it is with focus groups, where the researcher has latitude about the degree of "focus" he or she brings to the group. In their earliest form, this focus was very tight. Robert Merton and his colleagues at Columbia University used focus groups to measure limited kinds of audience effects. Merton was a consultant on this military-sponsored work and developed the use of focus groups around this time (Lee, 2010, p. 3). Specifically, Merton and his colleagues used focus groups to measure the "effects" of particular kinds of propaganda. These studies were linked to so-called "morale" studies undertaken by the US Army as the US entered World War II. The goal was to understand how morale could be kept high in both military and civilians in the wake of World War I and its horrors. In fact, the denotative meaning of the term "focused" was the idea around which this work evolved in the research literature.

In a seminal 1946 article published in the *American Journal of Sociology*, Robert Merton and Patricia Kendall discussed the "focused interview" as an important new methodological innovation—one that would allow interviewers to gather specific information from participants around delimited topics. Merton and Kendall envisioned the focused interview as a space tightly defined by the researcher. In the focused interview,

> [p]ersons are known to have been involved in a *particular concrete situation*: they have seen a film, heard a radio program, read a pamphlet, article, or book; or have participated in a psychological experiment or in uncontrolled, but observed, social situation.
>
> (Merton and Kendall, 1946, p. 541)

"Equipped in advance with a content analysis, the interviewer can readily distinguish the objective facts of the case from the subjective definitions of the situation" (p. 541) and thus tightly control the content and flow of group talk accordingly.

The authors went on to provide several examples of the focused interview in practice. The examples draw largely from (then contemporary) World War II propaganda research. The goal in these interviews was to elicit responses from the subject, free from the directive influence of the interviewer. That is, the interviewer set the stage and delimited the context. But the goal was even more specific and constrained—to excavate specific, targeted response from the interviewees. The interview should be an "informal listening-post or 'clinic' or 'laboratory'"—not a "debating society or authoritarian arena in which the interviewer defines the situation" (p. 547). Clearly the focus group was not a dialogic setting for Merton. Still, although the interviewer clearly defined the parameters of the interview setting and context, he or she was advised to take a largely passive role in the discussion that followed. One sees a concern here with something like "data contamination" or a "Heisenberg effect." According to Merton, the focused interview should avoid these as far as possible—another indication of the positivist epistemological impulses that motivated this project.

In terms of method, the goal was to blur the line between quantitative and qualitative work—a distinction Merton and Kendall thought old and outworn even in the 1940s. Using focused interviews researchers could develop hypotheses that could later be systematically tested (p. 557). Or, alternatively, the focused interview could be used to interpret material gathered from experimental studies (p. 557). Merton and Kendall were indeed pioneers, and the world of research methods would not catch up to them for more than five decades with the emergence of "mixed methods" research (e.g. Creswell, 2002; Teddlie and Tashakkori, 2008). Their seminal article in 1946 was groundbreaking and would later turn into the book *The Focused Interview* (1956—the second edition was published in 1990), which would become a founding text for focus group research. The book itself begins with a four-step process for conducting the focused interview (p. 3). First, the researcher gathers participants who have been involved in "a particular situation" (e.g. seen a film of television show, read a book, took part in an experiment). Second, the researcher develops a set of hypotheses based on a "content or situational analysis" of the phenomena in question. Third, the researcher develops an "interview guide" to allow these hypotheses to be tested. Fourth and finally, the researcher tries to ascertain participants' "definitions of the situation" in the interview setting. For Merton and his co-authors, "[e]quipped in advance with an analysis of the situation, the interviewer can readily distinguish the objective facts of the case from the subjective definitions of the situation" (p. 4).

Rereading the article and book today is instructive. In particular, we are struck by the following—there is no discussion of "groups" at all in the article. All of the interview transcript examples are taken from individual respondents. There is no talk of interaction between and among participants. One is left to reconstruct the idea that these focused interviews could involve or not involve focus groups as we understand them today. Merton himself would barely remark on the issue when he was asked to comment on the development of focus groups some 40 years later. The key was the "focus" of the interview as developed above—the number of participants involved was secondary. *The Focused Interview* does address the question of "the group"—but only briefly and towards the end of the book (Chapter 7). Even here, Merton and his colleagues are tentative, pointing to potential affordances of conducting the "focused interview" in a group. An obvious advantage, they note, is the diversity of responses. But, they add a caveat:

> Little enough is firmly known about the systemic differences between the types of data provided by interviews with individuals and with groups. It is not at all certain that the private interview is uniformly preferable to the interview with groups. It may even develop, on further study of this problem, that the group interview is preferable to the individual interview for certain types of problems.
>
> (Merton, 1990, pp. 135–136)

At the risk of becoming redundant, this last point is worth underscoring. The pioneers of focus group work were not particularly concerned about the potential advantages of studying "the group." Rather, they were concerned with the role of the interviewer and the "focus" of the interview—the ability to define a situation objectively and to gather the responses of many individuals to that situation. For Merton and others, the radical breakthrough was the notion that interviews could be targeted and focused around a specific "concrete situation" in order to achieve more focus and to delimit the kinds of information participants were likely to share. By Merton's own admission, the size of the interview was a secondary concern. In fact, he claimed that focus groups—in particular, the breakthrough of the "focus" in interview research—would help bridge the gap between qualitative and quantitative approaches to research. Yet, a closer examination reveals an abiding positivist orientation that would remain the legacy of much of this work. According to Merton and Kendall (1946), focus groups could generate "hypotheses" that could later be "submitted to systematic tests." Alternatively, focus groups could help "*interpret previously ascertained experimental findings*" (p. 557). In both of these cases, developing the "focus" in the "focused interview" allowed for commensurability and dialogue with experimental work. Merton's effort here was to give researchers tools to accumulate findings that could grow and develop in linear fashion—getting us closer, it seems, to deep and irrefutable truths. The "focus" in "focus group" was a fundamentally important tool for this methodological breakthrough.

The group

The original meaning and use of the term "group" in "focus group" was highly specific. Merton and others carefully gathered random samples from multiple populations to help measure the effects of propaganda messages. These were not self-organized groups or groups with shared interests or experiences or purposefully selected groups. They did not have an identity outside of the research context. In fact, the term "focus group" as opposed to "focused interview" or "focused group interview" only emerged during the 1960s (Lee, 2010) and largely in the field of marketing. The term was linked to the emergence of the professional market researcher. As Raymond Lee suggests, the term probably emerged from the everyday practice of such marketers. Its history is not well documented, embedded in the archives (if at all) of corporate sponsors such as those of the tobacco industry. Lee argued that the dramatic resurgence of focus group work in the 1970s might likely be linked to the shrinking economy and limited resources at marketing firms. Lee also gestured toward a theme that hangs over all such work—the supposed cost-efficiency of focus group work. This would long be an attraction of focus group work for many—but one with significant drawbacks as well. Focus groups have been seen as a way to do more interviews faster and in a more cost-efficient manner. Viewing and using focus group in this way precludes exploiting their unique affordances—affordances we discuss in detail in Chapter 3.

As Lee made clear, focus groups were heavily utilized by marketers and other corporate types with commercial interests. The applied nature of their work appealed to researchers and practitioners in the fields of "social marketing" and health promotion. Here, as well, focus group work blurred the line between research and application. For example, if the goal of the early cigarette studies was to understand attitudes towards smoking to perfect their advertising and sales, then the goal of "social marketing" was to promote the "social good" in whatever form it took. Drawing parallels between early marketing research and social marketing, Kotler and Zaltman (1971) wrote,

> [i]dentical reasoning is required by those who market altruistic causes (e.g. charity giving, blood donation), personal health causes (e.g. nonsmoking, better nutrition), and social betterment causes (e.g. civil rights, improved housing, better environment). In each case, the social marketer must define the change sought, which may be a change in values, beliefs, affects, behavior, or some mixture. He must meaningfully segment the target markets. He must design social products for each market that are 'buyable,' and that instru-mentally serve the social cause.
>
> (p. 7)

A decade later, Schearer (1981) constructed almost identical arguments about the use of focus groups in large-scale health promotion endeavors, including those around population control, cancer prevention, and breast feeding in developing countries. We see here the group treated as a "target market"—gauged for their attitudes, targeted for seemingly positive, social ends. Focus group research would continue to flourish in marketing and health fields. Both of these areas are of course largely "applied"—that is, they define their goals and outcomes a priori. Focus groups in these fields are not dialogic, nor are they co-constituted by facilitators and participants.

Since the early 1980s, focus group work would continue to flourish but the interest in "the group" and its affordances would proliferate, especially in "audience" or "reception" research studies. The primary goal of these kinds of studies was to understand the complexities involved in how people understood and interpreted media texts, and its data collection and analysis methods were almost exclusively qualitative. More specifically and in contrast to the work of Merton and colleagues, which focused primarily on expressed content, audience analysis researchers focused on group dynamics themselves because they believed that both the meanings constructed within groups of viewers and the viewers themselves were largely socially constructed. Some of the most important audience or reception studies include those that focused on the television show *Nationwide* in the UK (Morley, 1980), the television show *Dallas* in the Netherlands (Ang, 1985) and also in Israel (Liebes and Katz, 1990), and Janice Radway's (1984) classic study of women reading romance novels.

In a groundbreaking early study, David Morley (1980) attempted to chart all the various ways in which viewing groups from different social and economic classes responded to the popular television show *Nationwide*. He conducted content analyses of many episodes of the show, and he collected and analyzed data from focus groups conducted with people who had just watched these episodes. Working from within a social constructionist framework (e.g. Berger and Luckmann, 1966), his use of focus groups was strategic: "The choice to work with groups rather than individuals . . . was made on the grounds that much individually based interview research is flawed by a focus on individuals as social atoms divorced from their social context" (p. 97). In contrast to individual interviews, for Morley and other scholars interested in audience reception practices, focus groups are invaluable because they afford insights into how meanings get constructed *in situ*. In discussing his own work Morley noted,

> the aim was to discover how interpretations were collectively constructed through talk and the interchange between respondents in the group situation— rather than to treat individuals as the autonomous repositories of a fixed set of individual 'opinions' isolated from their social context
>
> (Morley, 1980, p. 97)

Morley and others would re-conceptualize the notion of "the group" in "focus group." While drawing on the tools of early propaganda research and other kinds of media "effects" studies, Morley and others also broadened the scope and use of these tools. We see here the audience treated not as a "target market" but a collective having its own particular autonomies and dynamic potentials for meaning construction and use. The goal of audience reception studies was to create situations that were as close as possible to how people actually interacted naturally with fellow viewers of particular media. Underpinning this orientation is a social constructivist epistemology—one that views the reception process—both of individuals and of groups—as dynamic and emergent.

Another trajectory of work would also challenge narrow notions of "applied" social research—the literacy "study circles" of Brazilian pedagogue Paulo Freire. Conducted in poor, rural areas of Brazil in the 1970s, Freire organized collective discussions meant to elicit words (and concomitant ideas) fundamentally important to the lives of illiterate adults. He called these "generative words." Working with several colleagues, he spent long periods of time in communities trying to understand community members' interests, investments, and concerns in order to elicit comprehensive sets of such words. These words were then used as starting points for literacy learning, and literacy learning was deployed in the service of social and political activism. Importantly, this use of "focus groups" differs considerably from the uses we have discussed so far. The topics for discussion come from the stakeholders themselves. The facilitators are non-directive. The Truth is not considered to be "out there" to be discovered but a phenomenon that emerges through dialogue or collective conversation. This empirical material demands a different set of analytic tools, tools that cannot be simply imported from one-on-one interviews. One needs to consider the group itself as the primary unity of analysis—not as a large group of individual interviews but as its own entity with its own autonomies and potentials. The implications of these ideas for data collection will be taken up most fully in Chapter 3.

We can see—even with this brief and incomplete history—that the nature and functions of focus groups have proliferated in several directions at once. In some iterations, the "focus" is dictated tightly by the interviewer. In others, the focus is constructed in dialogue among the participants. In some iterations, the "group" is irrelevant. In others, it is constitutive. In some iterations, the audience is constructed as a "market segment." In others, the audience is seen to be active and constructive. In still others, these boundaries begin to dissolve with the group as a dynamic social entity gaining increasing prominence and importance. In addition, we see focus group work move across considerably different domains of inquiry, domains that will eventually criss-cross and even cross-fertilize each other. We see the focus group method of gathering information taken up by everyone from corporate marketers to Marxist pedagogues. In sum, focus groups have constantly been in motion during the past six or more decades. They have moved across epistemologies, from positivism and post-positivism to social constructivism and poststructuralism. They have moved across disciplines, from sociology to media studies to education. Finally, they have moved across various domains, from the military to the corporate world to the health sciences to the academy. The concerns and tensions that characterized the earliest focus group research still register today. And a host of additional concerns, tensions, and imagined potentials have proliferated and continue to proliferate. Given this complex and variegated inquiry landscape, the researcher is forced to re-imagine his or her role in focus group work in fundamental ways.

Appropriation and use of focus groups in applied fields

This book arrives at a particular moment in history—a moment when cross-disciplinary discussions around method are exploding. Over the past few decades, "qualitative inquiry" has emerged as a trans-disciplinary discourse. Journals, conferences, handbooks, and other dissemination venues now draw together researchers from across the social sciences and humanities and engage them in rich and complex discussions about method and methodology. Such discussions are firmly embedded in contemporary theoretical debates, allowing broader conversations between scholars and researchers in and between disciplinary spaces.

As with many qualitative research approaches and strategies, there is a small and growing "cottage industry" of texts on focus groups. These include *Defining Focus Groups* (Barbour, 2008), *Focus Groups in Social Research* (Bloor et al., 2001), and *Focus Groups: A Practical Guide for Applied Research* (Kreuger and Casey, 2008). Like much work on qualitative methodology in general, these texts are largely practical "how to" guides. Although such texts and approaches are useful, they typically lack historical and theoretical grounding. One of the things we try to do in this book is to redress this problem. Perhaps most notably, we try to situate the many very good practical discussions of focus group inquiry within broader historical and theoretical lines of thought and practice. We do not treat focus groups as an "add on" to other kinds of qualitative data collection techniques, but as a methodological strategy with its own historical and theoretical specificity.

Focus groups remain the purview of applied areas of inquiry, such as nursing and the health sciences, counseling, marketing, and education. Although we have been using the term "applied" throughout, it is perhaps worth reflecting upon this term a bit here. Applied research is typically concerned with solving real world problems. These problems and their solutions are often largely prefigured in advance. In other words, the research involves some preferred, a priori, outcome. For example, the earliest work with focus groups was concerned with developing effective propaganda for the US during World War II. Subsequently, marketers and advertisers have used focus groups to market and sell their products most effectively. Much of the more academic work using focus groups has been applied as well—to conduct needs assessments or develop and implement programs of one kind or another (e.g. curriculum in education or wellness protocols in the health fields).

In this regard, research using focus groups in most healthcare fields, especially nursing, has increased dramatically during the past several decades. Tipping (1998) emphasized the use of focus groups as a method of "needs assessment" in health education. Wyatt, Krauskopf, and Davidson (2008) noted that focus groups can be usefully used for "program planning and evaluation" for school nurses. The idea that focus group research allows health practitioners to gather information to use to improve their practice is echoed throughout the literature in journals such as *Journal of School Nursing*, *Nurse Researcher*, and *Qualitative Health Research*. In fact, *Nurse Researcher* devoted a special issue to focus groups in 2007. The issue's editorial introduction contextualized the articles in the issue in an interesting, even surprising, way—calling focus groups "useful" but noting their limitations, especially their small sample size and the attendant dangers of generalization without adequate warrant (Parahoo, 2007). Parahoo also questioned whether focus groups can be a "stand alone method," noting that they can serve non-research purposes such as curriculum planning or reaching consensus. Echoing the likes of Merton and his colleagues, Parahoo also noted that focus groups can also be used "to develop tools such as questionnaires or interview schedules, to clarify and explore the findings from other methods" (Parahoo, 2007, p. 5). A clear subtext of his breezy introduction is that focus groups are largely subordinate to other research methods for nurses. In one article in the issue, Happell picked up these concerns, noting the large number of studies in nursing that now use focus groups (according to her count, 1176 between 1985 and 2004, with 781 between 2000 and 2004). She calls the use of focus groups a growing "fad" but notes the "need for more detail regarding the rationale for the use of focus groups than is currently being provided" (Happell, 2007, p. 23). Nearly all the other articles in this issue also advocate this cautious approach to focus group work—noting its limited uses for gauging attitudes and beliefs and its drawbacks vis-à-vis other (read: harder and more rigorous) kinds of methods.

Focus groups have also been widely used recently in counseling and counseling education. A 2007 article in the *Journal of Counseling and Development* by Kress and Shoffner remarked that focus groups "are becoming a popular research approach that counselors use as an efficient, practical, and applied method of gathering information to better serve clients" (p. 189). In the *Journal of Educational & Psychological Consultation*, Nabors et al. (2001) wrote that focus groups could serve as an "effective method for examining stakeholders' perception of mental health programs for children and their families" (p. 243). As in the health science fields, focus groups are largely used in counseling psychology to assess client needs and to develop programmatic interventions—their "benefits and areas for improvement" (p. 243).

In addition, focus groups are often used to research ostensibly sensitive topics and vulnerable populations in counseling-type settings. Supplementing survey work, for example, Hopson and Steiker (2008) used focus groups to explore drug abuse prevention programs in alternative schools. Similarly, Nelson-Gardell (2001) used focus groups to explore survivors of childhood sexual abuse, including who or what helped them cope (or not) with the abuse. And Briller et al. (2007/2008) used focus groups in a study of bereavement, noting the "special considerations" that need to be taken into account with this vulnerable population. Like most such studies, this one was largely concerned with how to implement focus groups most effectively and sensitively.

Whereas nursing and counseling psychology are applied fields within which focus groups have been used primarily for program development and implementation purposes, marketing—as a commercial enterprise and as an academic field—has long drawn on focus group research for needs assessments purposes—to determine the needs and desires of consumers and clients. According to Lee (2010), much of the history of this work is forever embedded in the proprietary files of advertising agencies. In the academic literature, however, this work has often involved comparing research that used focus groups with research that used other methods. For example, in "A Critical Comparison of Offline Focus Groups, Online Focus Groups and E-Delphi," Brüggen and Willems (2009) noted the rise in online marketing research and offered evidence to underscore the "deep outcomes" that emerge from what they call "offline focus groups." In a study reported in the *Journal of Foodservice Business Research*, York et al. (2009) similarly compared survey research to focus group research in studies designed to assess employee beliefs and practices around food safety. The goal of this research was to develop more effective workplace training around practices such as hand washing and cleaning food preparation surfaces, and the authors reported that focus group data were invaluable for these purposes. Some academic marketing researchers have sought to understand more fully technical or pragmatic aspects of focus group work. In an article in the *International Journal of Market Research*, for example, Tuckel and Wood (2001) investigated the ways respondents are (or are not) "cooperative" in focus group processes. Because participation in focus groups often involves monetary compensation, the danger that a cadre of "professional" respondents will develop is an issue. This work on why and how people participate in focus groups thus reanimates the idea that groups are little more than large numbers of individuals and thus reinvokes the Enlightenment epistemological concerns and anxieties we discussed earlier in relation to the work of Robert Merton and others during the 1940s.

As we have shown so far, focus groups have been deployed within a wide range of practitioner or applied fields. Education is another such field. Like the above examples, scholars in education have long used focus group work to assess and evaluate programs and curricula. For example, Peters (2009) demonstrated how focus groups were used to revise the Masters of Public Administration curricula at Western Michigan University. Like many other studies we have discussed in this section, this study employed mixed methods—survey, focus groups, and assessment measures. Similarly, Hall, Williams, and Daniel (2010) used focus groups to assess the effectiveness of an afterschool program for disadvantaged youth. In both of these cases (and others), focus groups have been used to evaluate the effectiveness of particular interventions by gauging the attitudes, dispositions, and outcomes of participants or stakeholders. Importantly, focus groups are central to the pedagogical interests of other applied fields—counselor education, nursing education, medical school education, business education and the like. In all of these fields, that inquiry and pedagogy are often linked is both well understood and utilized.

This brief and incomplete history shows that focus groups have been and still are widely used across many applied fields. This history also shows that both theory and research around focus groups continue to revisit many of the conceptual and practical issues raised by the earliest researchers to use focus groups—the use of focus groups for needs assessment and program development and implementation, the subordination of focus groups data to quantifiable data, and struggles to understand the nature and functions of "groups" as more than collections of individuals. Despite their widespread use in many fields for many decades, focus group research remains under-theorized and under-utilized.

This chapter and this book begin to redress this situation. In particular, we try to give shape and voice to the various ways focus groups have been appropriated and used. To do this, we focus on three key functions—the pedagogical, the political, and the empirical. We highlight the ways that focus group work has been used in the service of each of these functions, as well as how multiple functions have often been a part of much focus group work. As we will argue in subsequent chapters, these functions are seldom related in simple, unproblematic ways. Political interventions, for example, do not necessarily emerge from research inquiry. And when they do, this often occurs in unexpected or unintended ways. Similarly, pedagogy is not always central to activist work, but it can be and often is. Within any given project, these different dimensions or functions of focus group work emerge and interact in distinct and often disjunctive ways, eventually resulting in some unique interactive stabilizations. Although not entirely unique to research that utilizes focus groups, these dynamic relations, again, tend to occur more often with focus groups than with many other data collection strategies (e.g. individual conversational interviews, participant observation).

Structure and content of this book

This chapter introduced the reader to focus groups. We highlighted their origins, their earliest tensions, as well as continuities and discontinuities in their use over time. In Chapter 2, few argue that focus groups can be seen as having several parallel histories. We also show how focus groups have been put to several uses over the past century or so. The US military (e.g. Robert Merton), multi-national corporations (e.g. Proctor & Gamble), Marxist revolutionaries (e.g. Paulo Freire), literacy activists (e.g. Jonathan Kozol), and three waves of feminist scholar-activists (e.g. Esther Madriz), among others, have all used focus groups to help advance their specific concerns and causes.

In Chapter 3, we explore the particular affordances of focus group work. Taking seriously the performative turn in qualitative research, we pay particular attention to the kinds of knowledge and experience that focus group work seems to be able to draw out better than most other data collection strategies. These include: mitigating the researcher's authority and generating deeper understandings;

disclosing the constitutive power of discourse and the lifeblood of social activity; approximating the natural; filling in knowledge gaps and saturating understanding; drawing out complexity, nuance, and contradiction; disclosing eclipsed or invisible connections; and creating opportunities for solidarity building and political action. Taken together, these affordances allow us a sharper angle of vision on the specificities and autonomies of focus group research.

In Chapter 4, we offer general advice for using focus groups based on our own experiences. This chapter brings the reader closer to "the ground" in terms of understanding focus group work. Based on our own empirical work, we highly recommend certain practices for conducting focus groups because they contribute to dialogic, synergistic interactions that produce rich complex data. These include: expecting, even celebrating, unpredictable group dynamics, conflict, and contradiction; exploiting pre-existing social networks that encourage collegiality; creating safe, comfortable, and even festive spaces "of" the people; using open-ended prompts for questions and then letting group participants direct the flow of talk and social interaction; keeping notes and following up on key themes and gaps; listening for *breakdowns* and *subtexts* and asking for elaboration; and trying to create openings for social solidarity and political synergy.

To ground this more "practical" discussion, we use transcript data from focus groups we have conducted in our own work. These include focus groups with Mexican American women around learning English, healthcare, and transportation, and focus groups conducted with black youth around hip hop and film. We present and analyze transcripts both to illuminate the previous discussion about effective focus group work and also to begin a discussion about the data generated from focus group work and how to analyze them. Indeed, this will be the first volume to explore "data collection" and focus group research through analytic categories particular to such work. We thus highlight the particular kinds of data that emerge from focus groups—data distinct from the kinds gathered using one-on-one interviews or observations. In parallel fashion, we discuss the theories of self at work in focus groups as distinct from those at work in individual interviews.

Finally, in Chapter 5, we examine contemporary threats to focus group work. We also discuss new research frontiers where focus groups are likely to be quite useful and where the very nature of these frontiers is likely to expand our understandings of the nature and functions of focus group work. Focus groups are increasingly under new kinds of surveillance (from Institutional Review Boards [IRBs], funding agencies, publication venues, etc.). Key here is the notion of *anonymity*. The kind of anonymity that concerns IRBs can usually be preserved in one-on-one interviews if the interviewer adheres to given protocols. Yet, in group settings, trust and a commitment to confidentiality are more widely distributed and thus less controllable. We discuss the ways we must often educate key gatekeepers about focus groups and their particular affordances. In short, one must argue why and how the potential risk of participants violating commitments to anonymity are outweighed by the unique kinds of information that could only be gathered from group interviews.

With respect to new frontiers, we focus primarily on the ways that new information technologies seem to be changing the possibilities for focus group configurations and potentials of focus group activity. Among the issues we discuss in this section include: differences between synchronous and asynchronous online discussion groups; ways in which online focus groups can enhance research efficiency; anonymity (especially when with visual media); differences between text-only and text plus video virtual focus groups; increased potential for discourteous or deviant behavior in virtual environments; enhanced capacities for full disclosure, especially in text-only online environments; and whether and how virtual focus groups might rearticulate the functions and affordances we discuss in Chapters 2 and 3.

Conclusions

This book addresses, and even tries to integrate, historical, conceptual, theoretical, and practical issues. As noted above, much of the published work on focus groups to date has been devoted primarily to their practical or applied dimensions. The artificial separation of theory from practice has elided discussions that can advance more systematic understandings of the nature and potentials of focus groups. In this book, we draw together ideas that begin to constitute a foundation for advancing richer discussions of focus group work. We look to three alternative genealogies of focus group work—the pedagogical, the political, and the empirical. We pull these apart, put them back together, and highlight the work that they do. We also share what we believe to be quasi-unique affordances of focus groups and focus group work. The goal throughout is to advance a set of understandings about focus group work that attends to its radical particularity as a research tool—especially in relation to the collection of empirical material.

Chapter 2

Multiple, interrelated functions of focus group work

In the last chapter, we explored the origins of focus group work as it is currently understood. We highlighted the fact that the "focused interview" was a breakthrough in social scientific work, as well as its prolific uptake across a wide variety of applied fields. These include nursing and the health professions, counseling, marketing, and education. We also noted that, in most cases, focus group work has been put in the service of normative or a priori outcomes—to assess the needs of communities, to devise ways to implement policies, to assess consumer response to products, and so on. We also noted that much of focus group work has evolved in an ad hoc and haphazard manner. Finally, we emphasized the fact that many of the basic principles and practices of the earliest focus group work remain with us to this day. For example, focus groups are still often conceptualized (in practice) as large group interviews. Focus groups are also still often used primarily to complement quantifiable data from surveys, quantitative assessment instruments, and the like, or to help interpret and explain quantitative findings. Given these and other residues of history, we believe that the full potentialities of focus group work remain un-mined.

In this chapter, we provide accounts of what we believe to be three primary functions of focus group work: the pedagogical, the political, and the empirical. In doing so, we attempt to give shape to a set of unwieldy histories, often embedded in the practicalities of applied work. Inspired by Laurel Richardson's (2000) image of the crystal as productive for mapping the changing complexity of the lives of her research participants and her own life as a sociologist, we find the image of the prism to be useful for re-visioning the primary functions of focus group work (pedagogy, politics, and inquiry), as well as the relations between and among them. We attempt to give a history to the various and applied lineages.

A prism is a transparent optical element with flat, polished surfaces that can both refract and reflect light. The most common use of the term "prism" refers to a triangular prism—one that has a triangular base and three clear rectangular surfaces. When viewed from different angles, one can see more or less of each of its three surfaces. From some angles, for example, one surface is completely and directly visible with the other two surfaces partially and obliquely visible. From other angles, two surfaces are completely visible with the third surface visible but obliquely and in the distance. Importantly, however, from every angle of vision, at least some of every surface is visible. From some angles, prisms break up light into its constituent spectral colors. From other angles, they act like mirrors, reflecting all or almost all approaching light back toward its source. Similarly, all three focus group functions are always at work simultaneously; they are all visible to the researcher to some extent; and they all both refract and reflect the content of focus group work in different ways.

These three functions are seldom related in simple, unproblematic ways. Political interventions, for example, do not necessarily emerge from inquiry. Or they might emerge from inquiry in unexpected or unintended ways. Similarly, pedagogy is not always central to activist work, but it can be and often is. Within any given project, these different dimensions or functions of focus group work emerge and interact in distinct and often disjunctive ways, eventually resulting in some unique interactive stabilization. We will touch upon this disjunctive emergence in our discussions of different lines of work within which one or another of these functions has been framed as dominant. Drawing on these histories of focus group work, we alert the readers to insights that flow from these several unique functions. The *pedagogical* surface of focus group work alters us to the dialogic nature of focus group interaction, as well as the possibility for transformative encounters. The *political* surface of focus group work alerts us to the sources of collective support that can occur around social and political issues, as well as the dangers of naïve notions of collectivity. The *empirical* (or inquiry) surface of focus group work alerts us to the deep epistemological issues and concerns around "the research act," including the complex negotiations between "self" and "other" in inquiry.

The pedagogical surface of focus group work: Paulo Freire and beyond

In this section, we highlight how focus groups have been important pedagogical sites/instruments throughout history. Acknowledging that there are a plethora of historical examples of pedagogically motivated focus groups—from dialogues in the fifth century BC Athenian Square to early African American book clubs to union-sponsored "study circles" to university study groups—we foreground the focus groups cultivated by Paulo Freire in Brazil. Through analyses of some of his work, we show how collective critical literacy practices were used to address local politics and concerns for social justice. Among other things, we foreground the ways in which Freire worked *with* people and not *on* them, thus modeling an important praxis disposition for contemporary educators and qualitative researchers (e.g. Barbour and Kitzinger, 1999). Pedagogy, in Freire's work, was the dominant function of focus groups. However, inquiry always nourished pedagogy and pedagogy was seen as useful only to the extent that it mobilized activist work.

Freire's work was intensely practical as well as deeply philosophical. His most famous book, *Pedagogy of the Oppressed* (1993/1970), can be read as equal parts social theory, philosophy, and pedagogical method. His claims about education are foundational, rooted both in his devout Christian beliefs and his commitment to Marxism. Throughout *Pedagogy of the Oppressed*, Freire argued that the goal of education is to begin to "name the world," part of which is to recognize that we are all "subjects" of our own lives and narratives, not "objects" in the stories of others. We must acknowledge the ways in which we, as human beings, are fundamentally charged with producing and transforming reality together. He argued further that those who do not acknowledge this, those who want to control and oppress, are committing a kind of symbolic violence.

Freire often referred to oppressive situations as "limit situations"—situations that people cannot imagine themselves beyond. Limit situations naturalize people's sense of oppression, giving it a kind of obviousness and immutability. As particularly powerful ideological state apparatuses, schools, of course, play a big role in this naturalization process. In this regard, Freire argued that most education is based on the "banking model" where educators see themselves as authoritative subjects, depositing knowledge into the minds of their students, their objects. This implies an Enlightenment worldview, where subject and object are a priori independent of each other, and where subjects are objectified and thus de-humanized. Among other things, the banking model of education implies that "the teacher teaches and the students are taught" and that "the teacher knows everything and the students know nothing" (Freire, 1993/1970, p. 54). The model operates according to monologic rather than dialogic logics, serving the interests of the status quo and functioning to promote business as usual rather than social change. As problematic as it is, the banking model provides the epistemological foundation for most contemporary educational institutions and practices.

To supplant a "banking model" of education, Freire offered up an alternative model that was based on the elicitation of words (and concomitant ideas) that are fundamentally important in the lives of the people for whom educational activities are designed. He called these words "generative words." He spent long periods of time in communities trying to understand community members' interests, investments, and concerns in order to elicit comprehensive sets of "generative words." These words were then used as starting points for literacy learning, and literacy learning was deployed in the service of social and political change. More specifically, "generative words" were paired with pictures that represented them and then interrogated by people in the community both for what they revealed and concealed with respect to the circulation of multiple forms of capital and extant power relations. Freire encouraged the people both to explore how the meanings and effects of these words functioned in their lives and to conduct research on how their meanings and effects did (or could) function in different ways in different social and political contexts. The primary goal of these activities was to help people feel in control of their words and to be able to use them to exercise power over the material and ideological conditions of their own lives. Thus, Freire's literacy programs were designed not so much to teach functional literacy but to raise people's critical consciousness (*conscientization*) and to encourage them to engage in "praxis" or critical reflection inextricably linked to political action in the real world. He was clear to underscore the fact that praxis is never easy and always involves power struggles, often violent ones.

The fact that Freire insisted that the unending process of emancipation must be a collective effort is far from trivial. Central to this process is a faith in the power of dialogue. Importantly, dialogue for Freire was defined as collective reflection/action. He believed that dialogue, fellowship, and solidarity are essential to human liberation and transformation.

> We can legitimately say that in the process of oppression someone oppresses someone else; we cannot legitimately say that in the process of revolution, someone liberates someone else, nor yet that someone liberates himself, but rather that men in communion liberate each other.
>
> (Freire, 1993/1970, p. 103)

Only dialogue is capable of producing critical consciousness and praxis. Thus, all educational programs (and especially all language and literacy programs) must be dialogic. They must be spaces wherein "equally knowing subjects" (p. 31) engage in collective struggle in efforts to transform themselves and their worlds.

Within Freireian pedagogies, the development and use of "generative" words and phrases and the cultivation of *conscientization* are enacted in the context of locally situated "study circles" (or focus groups). The goal for the educator within these study circles is to engage, with people, in their lived realities, producing and transforming them. Again, for Freire, this kind of activity was part and parcel of literacy programs always already grounded in larger philosophical and social projects, ones concerned with how people might more effectively "narrate" their own lives. In the context of these study circles, educators immerse themselves in the communities to which they have committed themselves. They try to enter into conversations, to elicit "generative" words and phrases together with their participants, and then to submit these words and phrases to intense reflection—presentation and re-presentation—in order to bring into relief lived contradictions that can then be acted upon.

To illustrate this kind of problem-posing education rooted in people's lived realities and contradictions, Freire created what would now be called collaborative research (CAR) or participatory action research (PAR) programs with participants, including one designed around the question of alcoholism. Because alcoholism was a serious problem in the city where Freire lived and worked, he and his research team showed assembled groups a photograph of a drunken man walking past three other men talking on the corner and asked them to talk about what was going on in the photograph. The groups responded, in effect, by saying that the drunken man was a hard worker, the only hard worker in the group, and he was probably worried about his low wages and having to support his family. In their words, "he is a decent worker and a souse like us" (Freire, 1993/1970, p. 99). The men in the study circles seemed to recognize themselves in this man, noting both that he was a "souse" but also situating his drinking in a politicized context. Alcoholism was "read" as a response to oppression and exploitation. The groups went on to discuss these issues. This example of problem-posing pedagogy is quite different from (and we would argue much more effective than) more didactic approaches such as "character education," which would more likely involve "sermonizing" to people about their failings. Problem-posing education is proactive and designed to allow the people themselves to identify and generate solutions to the problems they face. The goal is to de-code images and language in ways that eventually lead to questioning and transforming the material and social conditions of existence. Freire offered other examples as well, including showing people different (and contradictory) news stories covering the same event. In each case, the goal of problem-posing pedagogy is to help people understand the contradictions they live and to use these understandings to change their worlds.

In sum, focus group work has always been central to the kinds of radical pedagogies that have been advocated and fought for by intellectual workers like Paulo Freire and his many followers (e.g. Henry Giroux, Joe Kincheloe, Jonathan Kozol, and Peter McLaren). Organized around "generative" words and phrases and usually located within unofficial spaces, focus groups become sites of/for collective struggle and social transformation. As problem-posing formations, they operate locally to identify, interrogate, and change specific lived contradictions that have been rendered invisible by hegemonic power/knowledge regimes. Their operation also functions to re-route the circulation of power within hegemonic struggles and even to re-define what power is and how it works. Perhaps most importantly for our purposes here, the impulses that motivate focus groups in pedagogical domains or for pedagogical functions have important implications for re-imagining and using focus groups as resources for constructing "effective histories" (Foucault, 1984) within qualitative research endeavors.

Although we have highlighted the pedagogical function of Freire's use of study circles, pedagogy is only a contingently situated function. That is, the three functions noted above can—and almost always are—implicated in each other. Freire's study circles are excellent examples of the multifunctionality of focus groups. Though designed primarily as pedagogical activities, they were also inextricably linked to activist-based and research-oriented activities. Recall that a starting point for Freire's work was to investigate and unearth the key "generative" words and phrases that indexed key social problems in the Brazilian communities in which Freire worked—clearly a form of research. And of course, his pedagogy was entirely motivated by and imbricated in an activist agenda—helping rural Brazilians learn to de-code and then transform the world around them, especially its systemic oppressions.

The political surface of focus group work: Consciousness raising groups and beyond

In this section, we offer descriptions and interpretations of focus groups in the service of radical political work designed within social justice agendas. In particular, we focus on how the consciousness raising groups (CRGs) of second- and third-wave feminism have been deployed to mobilize empowerment agendas and to enact social change. This work complements and extends the explicitly pedagogical work we just discussed, especially in its ways of theorizing relations between the self and the social, its active investment in community empowerment agendas, and its commitment to praxis. It also provides important insights relevant for re-imagining the possibilities of focus group activity within qualitative research endeavors. Whereas Freire's primary goal was to use literacy (albeit broadly defined) to mobilize oppressed groups to work against their oppression through praxis, the primary goal of the CRGs of second- and third-wave feminism was to build theory from the lived experiences of women that could work towards their own emancipation. This is a subtle but important difference, and one that seems largely an effect of the very different social and political contexts in which Freire and second- and third-wave feminists worked.

In our discussion of CRGs here, we draw heavily on Esther Madriz's retrospective analyses of second-wave feminist work as well as her own third-wave feminist work. In both of these endeavors, Madriz focused on political (and politicized) uses of focus groups within qualitative inquiry, demonstrating that there has been a long history of deploying focus groups in consciousness raising activities and for promoting social justice agendas within feminist and womanist traditions. Importantly, as forms of collective testimony, focus group participation has often been empowering for women, especially women of color (Madriz, 2000, p. 843). This is the case for several reasons. Focus groups de-center the authority of the researcher, allowing women safe spaces to talk about their own lives and struggles. These groups also allow women to connect with each other collectively, to share their own experiences, and to "reclaim their humanity" in a nurturing context (p. 843). Very often, Madriz noted, women themselves take these groups over, re-conceptualizing them in fundamental ways and with simple yet far-reaching political and practical consequences. In this regard, Madriz argued that

> focus groups can be an important element in the advancement of an agenda of social justice for women, because they can serve to expose and validate women's everyday experiences of subjugation and their individual and collective survival and resistance strategies.
>
> (Madriz, 2000, p. 836)

> Group interviews are particularly suited for uncovering women's daily experience through collective stories and resistance narratives that are filled with cultural symbols, words, signs, and ideological representations that reflect different dimensions of power and domination that frame women's quotidian experiences.
>
> (Madriz, 2000, p. 839)

As such, these groups constitute spaces for generating collective "testimonies," and these testimonies help both individual women and groups of women find or produce their own unique and powerful "voices."

As Madriz and others have demonstrated, focus groups have multiple histories within feminist lines of thought and action. Soon after slavery ended in the United States, for example, churchwomen and teachers gathered to organize political work in the South (e.g. Gilkes, 1994). Similarly, turn of the century "book clubs" were key sites for intellectual nourishment and political work (e.g. Gere, 1987). Mexican women have always gathered in kitchens and at family gatherings to commiserate and to work together to better their lives (e.g. Behar, 1993; Dill, 1994). And in 1927, Chinese women working in the San Francisco garment industry held focus group discussions to organize against their exploitation, which eventually led to a successful strike (e.g. Espiritu, 1997). Although we do not unpack these and other complex histories in this chapter, we do offer general accounts of the nature and function of focus groups within second- and third-wave feminism in the United States. These accounts pivot on the examination of several original manifesto-like texts generated within the movement, which we offer as synecdoches of the contributions of a much richer, more complex, contradictory, and intellectually and politically "effective" set of histories.

Perhaps the most striking realization that emerges from examining some of the original texts of second-wave feminism are the explicitly self-conscious ways in which women used focus groups as "research" to build "theory" about women's everyday experiences and to deploy theory to enact political change. Interestingly but not surprisingly, this praxis-oriented work was dismissed by male radicals at the time as little more than "gossip" in the context of "coffee klatches." (Ironically, this dismissal mirrors the ways in which qualitative inquiry is periodically dismissed for being "soft" or "subjective" or non-scientific.") Nevertheless, second-wave feminists persisted in building theory from the "standpoint" of women's lived experiences, and their efforts eventually became a powerful social force in the struggle for equal rights.

In many respects, the CRGs of second-wave feminism helped set the agenda for the next generation of feminist activism. As Hester Eisenstein (1984) noted, these groups helped bring personal issues in women's lives to the forefront of political discourse. Abortion, incest, sexual molestation, and domestic and physical abuse, for example, emerged from these groups as pressing social issues around which public policy and legislation had to be enacted. Importantly, these issues had previously been considered too personal and too intensely idiosyncratic to be taken seriously by men at the time, whether they were scholars, political activists, or politicians. By finding out which issues were most pressing in women's lives, CRGs were able to articulate what had previously been considered individual, psychological and private matters to the agendas of local collectives and eventually to social and political agendas at regional and national levels.

Working within the movement(s) of third-wave feminism, Madriz herself used focus groups in powerful ways, some of which are evidenced in her 1997 book,

Nothing Bad Happens to Good Girls: Fear of Crime in Women's Lives. In this book, Madriz discussed all the ways in which the fear of crime works to produce an insidious form of social control on women's lives. Fear of crime produces ideas and dispositions about what women "should" and "should not" do in public to protect themselves, enabling debilitating ideas about what constitutes "good girls" verses "bad girls" and severely constraining the range of everyday practices available to women.

With respect to research methods, Madriz called attention to the fact that most research findings on women's fear of crime had previously been generated from large survey studies of both men and women. This approach, she argued, severely limits the range of thought and experience that participants are willing to share and thus leads both to inaccurate and partial accounts of the phenomenon under study. In other words, it is hard to get people—women in particular—to talk about sensitive topics such as their own fears of assault or rape in uninhibited and honest ways in the context of oral or written surveys completed alone or in relation to a single social scientist interviewer. This general problem is further complicated by differences in power relations between researchers and research participants that obtain as a function of age, social class, occupation, language proficiency, race and so on.

To work against the various alienating forces that seem inherent in survey research and to collect richer and more complex accounts of experience with greater verisimilitude, Madriz used focus groups, noting that these groups provided a context where women could support each other in discussing their experiences of and fears and concerns about crime. Indeed, these groups do mitigate the intimidation, fear, and suspicion with which many women experience the one-on-one interview. In the words of one of Madriz's participants, "when I am alone with an interviewer, I feel intimidated, scared. And if they call me over the telephone, I never answer their questions. How do I know what they really want or who they are?" (Madriz, 1997, p. 165). In contrast, focus groups afford women safer and more supportive contexts within which to explore their lived experiences and the consequences of these experiences with other women who will understand what they are saying intellectually, emotionally, and viscerally.

This idea of safe and supportive spaces ushers in another important dimension of focus group work within third-wave feminist research, namely the importance of constituting groups in ways that mitigate alienation, create solidarity, and enhance community building. To achieve such ends, Madriz argued for the importance of creating homogenous groups in terms of race, class, age, specific life experiences, and so on.

In relation to this point, CRGs of second-wave feminism suffered from essentializing tendencies (whether politically strategic or not) that ended up glossing the many, different, and even contradictory experiences of many women and groups of women under the singular sign of "woman." More importantly and also more problematically, this sign was constructed largely from the lived experiences of white middle-class women. Acknowledging the need to see and to celebrate more variability in this regard, third-wave feminist researchers refracted and multiplied the "standpoints" from which testimonies might flow and voices might be produced. Although many held onto the post-positivist ideal of "building theory" from lived experience, researchers like Madriz pushed for theory that accounted more fully for the local, complex, and nuanced nature of lived experience, which is always already constructed within intersections of power relations produced by differences between and among multiple social categories (e.g. race, ethnicity, national origin, class, gender, age, sexual orientation, etc.). In the end, a primary goal of focus group activity within third-wave feminist research is not to offer prescriptive conclusions but to highlight the productive potentials (both oppressive and emancipatory) of particular social contexts (with their historically produced and durable power relations) within which such prescriptions typically unfold. In this regard, the work of Madriz is a synecdoche for third-wave feminist work more broadly conceived—particularly work conducted by women of color such as Dorinne Kondo, Smadar Lavie, Ruth Behar, Aiwa Ong, and Lila Abu-Lughod.

The nature and functions of CRGs within second- and third-wave feminism offer many important insights into the potentials of focus group work. Building upon Madriz's political reading of focus groups, and more specifically on the constructs of *testimony* and *voice*, we now highlight some of these potentials. One key purpose of focus groups within feminist work has been to elicit and validate collective testimonies and group resistance narratives. Women use such testimonies and narratives "to unveil specific and little-researched aspects of women's daily existences, their feelings, attitudes, hopes, and dreams" (Madriz, 2000, p. 836). Another key emphasis of focus groups within feminist and womanist traditions has been the discovery or production of *voice*. Because focus groups often result in the sharing of similar stories of everyday experience, struggle, rage, and the like, they often end up validating individual voices that had previously been constructed within and through mainstream discourses as idiosyncratic, selfish, and even evil. Because they foreground and exploit the power of testimony and voice, focus groups can become sites for overdetermining collective identity as strategic political practice—to create a critical mass of visible solidarity that seems a necessary first step toward social and political change.

Focus groups within feminist and womanist traditions have also mitigated the Western tendency to separate thinking and feeling, thus opening up possibilities for re-imagining knowledge as distributed, relational, embodied, and sensuous. Viewing knowledge in this light brings into relief the complexities and contradictions that are always involved in field work. It also brings into view the relations between power and knowledge and thus insists that qualitative research is always already political—implicated in social critique and social change.

Either out of necessity or for strategic purposes, feminist work has always taken the constitutive power of *space* into account. To further work against asymmetrical power relations and the processes of "othering," meetings are almost always held in safe spaces where women feel comfortable, important, and validated. This is a particularly important consideration when working with women who have much to lose from their participation such as undocumented immigrants, victims of abuse, or so-called deviant youth.

Finally, the break from second-wave to third-wave feminism both called into question the monolithic treatment of difference under the sign of "woman" that characterized much of second-wave thinking and also highlighted the importance of creating focus groups that are relatively "homogeneous" in terms of life histories, perceived needs, desire, race, social class, region, age, and so forth because such groups are more likely to achieve the kind of solidarity and collective identity requisite for producing "effective histories" (Foucault, 1984). Although coalition building across more heterogeneous groups of women may be important in some instances, focused intellectual and political work is often most successful when enacted by people with similar needs, desires, struggles, and investments.

Politicized forms of focus group work are perhaps best evidenced today in various PAR projects. In the United States, Michelle Fine has helped form various "research collectives" with youth at the City University of New York (CUNY) Graduate Center over the past few years, around several contemporary social issues (Cammarota and Fine, 2008). For example, Fine brought together multi-ethnic groups of suburban and urban high schools for *Echoes of Brown* (with Roberts and Torre, 2004), a study of the legacies of Brown versus Board of Education. Originally a study of the so-called "achievement gap," the framework soon shifted, due largely to the focus group-like sessions that drew the participants together: "At our first session, youth from six suburban high schools and three urban high schools immediately challenged the frame of our research" (Torre and Fine, 2006, p. 273). After discussion, the framework changed from one of the "achievement gap"—a construct the youth felt put too much of the onus on themselves—to the "opportunity gap."

These research collectives opened up spaces for youth to challenge themselves and others in ongoing dialogue—a key affordance of focus group work, as noted above. "As we moved through our work, youth were able to better understand material, or to move away from experiences that were too uncomfortable, or to make connections across seemingly different positions" (Torre and Fine, 2006, p. 276). Ultimately, these youth were able to carry out both empirical projects around "push out rates" and disciplinary practices in schools as well as to produce powerful individual and collective testimonies about their own perspectives on and experiences of schooling, 50 years after Brown. Key here was the PAR "under construction" principle, the idea that opinions, ideas, beliefs, and practices are always expected to change and grow (Torre and Fine, 2006, p. 274). See Cammarota and Fine (2008) for additional examples of this principle at work.

While Fine and others have done their work largely in the US, Torre and Fine have linked PAR explicitly to histories of worldwide political struggle.

> Based largely on the theory and practice of Latino activist scholars, PAR scholars draw from neo-Marxist, feminist, queer, and critical race theory . . .

to articulate methods and ethics that have local integrity and stretch topo-
graphically to site/cite global patters on domination and resistance.

(Torre and Fine, 2006, p. 271)

They have analyzed and discussed the work of Columbian sociologist Fals Borda
in great detail. Borda is considered by many to be the "founder" of PAR. In their
efforts to re-map PAR from a global perspective, Torre and Fine have underscored
the international scope of focus group work, particularly around their political uses
and with the use of many exemplary PAR efforts across the globe.

Indeed, if we look around the world, we quickly realize that the original impulses
of feminist consciousness raising work have been taken up and re-inflected in
multiple ways and for many purposes within various PAR initiatives. In Australia,
for example, the "Deadly Maths Consortium" created by Thomas Cooper and
Annette Barturo is a PAR project that has been extraordinarily effective in improving
mathematics learning among indigenous peoples (e.g. Cooper et al., 2008). In New
Zealand, Russell Bishop has worked both tirelessly and very successfully to enact
PAR initiatives designed to create collaborations based on caring relationships where
power is shared among self-determining individuals within non-dominating
relations of interdependence; where cultural traditions matter; where learning is
dialogic; where participants are connected to one another through the establishment
of a common vision for what constitutes excellence in educational outcomes—all
characteristics that are paramount to the educational performance of Maori students
(e.g. Bishop et al., 2006). And indigenous scholars in the United States have used
various forms of collaborative and participatory action research to work against the
effects of colonization and to pursue their own liberation collectively and
systematically (e.g. Grand, 2004; Wilson and Yellow Bird, 2005).

We have highlighted here the political function of focus groups—the ways these
groups allow participants to coalesce around key issues, co-producing knowledges
and strategies for transcending their social, economic, and political circumstances.
As noted throughout, however, other functions are almost always embedded in
projects where the dominant purposes or function is political. For example, the
political theory building and practice we have emphasized relies on the kinds of
critical, pedagogical practices associated with Freire and others. (In fact, Torre and
Fine also explicitly link PAR to the work of Freire.) The interactions between
participants in consciousness raising and other feminist groups, for example, are
deeply pedagogical, as knowledge is co-created in situated and dialogic ways.
Finally, these groups often engage in inquiry, especially inquiry focused on
understanding asymmetrical power relations that render both women and
particular groups of women as inferior in any number of ways. Although they have
often been caricatured as uncritical support groups, consciousness raising and other
feminist groups have always been intensely concerned with producing new and
useful knowledge about issues such as domestic violence or rape or workplace
marginalization that were often broadly misconstrued within "official knowledge"

regimes of truth. And the PAR work we have mentioned continues to build upon and extend the productive linkages among pedagogy, politics, and inquiry.

Michelle Fine's notion of "strong objectivity" is helpful in this regard. According to Fine, we must work toward new forms of objectivity informed by the insights and advances of critical scholarship—particularly scholarship about the "situatedness" of all knowledge. For Fine, this reflection can be a source of better, more honest, and more "objective" accounts of our work. Drawing on the work of Sandra Harding, Fine argued that "strong objectivity" is "achieved when researchers work aggressively through their own positionality, values, and predispositions, gathering as much evidence as possible, from many distinct vantage points, all in an effort not to be guided, unwittingly, by predispositions and the pull of biography" (Fine, 2006). Such an approach helps researchers become more aware of potential "blind spots" that they may import, unwittingly and not, to their studies. Such work can be usefully done in "work groups," where empirical material can be discussed, pulled apart, and cleared of the fog of unacknowledged subjectivities. These work groups seem to share the best impulses of focus group work, as participants forge new kinds of understandings and try to avoid premature closure. These impulses allow us to interrogate how focus groups can foster approaches to political work that challenge the notion of "collectivity" itself.

The inquiry surface of focus group work: From positivism to poststructuralism and beyond

As noted in the last chapter, the interest in focus groups in the social sciences has ebbed and flowed during the past 60 or so years. In many respects, the first really visible use of focus groups for conducting social science research may be traced back to the work of Paul Lazarsfeld and Robert Merton. Their focus group approach emerged in 1941, as the pair embarked on a government-sponsored project to assess media effects on attitudes toward America's involvement in World War II. Working within the Office of Radio Research at Columbia University, they recruited groups of people to listen and respond to radio programs designed to boost "morale" for the war effort (e.g. Merton, 1987, p. 552). Originally, the pair asked participants to push buttons to indicate their satisfaction or dissatisfaction with the content of the radio programs. Because the data yielded from this work could help them answer "what" questions but not "why" questions about participants' choices, they used focus groups as forums for getting participants to explain why they responded in the ways that they did. Importantly, Lazarsfeld and Merton's use of focus group strategies for data collection always remained secondary to (and less legitimate than) the various quantitative strategies they also used. In other words, they used focus groups in exploratory ways to generate new questions that could be operationalized in quantitative work or simply to complement or annotate the findings yielded from their mostly large-scale survey studies.

In philosophy of science terms, the early use of focus groups as resources for conducting research was highly conservative in nature. This is not at all surprising when we consider that the work of Lazarsfeld and Merton was funded by the military and included "interviewing groups of soldiers in Army camps about their responses to specific training films and so-called morale films" (Merton, 1987, p. 554). Their research also included many other media reception studies on topics such as why people made war bond pledges or how people responded to government-sponsored advertisements. The goal of most of this work was use knowledge about people's beliefs and decision-making processes to develop increasingly effective forms of propaganda—inquiry in the service of politics.

Although both their goals and the techniques merit harsh criticism (especially from progressive and radical camps), two key ideas from Lazarsfeld and Merton's work have become central to the legacy of using focus groups within qualitative research: (a) capturing people's responses in real time and space in the context of face-to-face interactions; and (b) strategically generating interview prompts *in situ* based on themes that are generated in these face-to-face interactions and that are considered particularly important to researchers.

The kind of focus group research conducted by scholars such as Lazarsfeld and Merton continued as a powerful force within corporate sponsored market research, but it all but disappeared within the field of sociology in the middle-part of the twentieth century, only to re-emerge in the early 1980s in the form of "audience analysis" research. When it did re-emerge, it was no longer wed to (or used in the service of) predominantly quantitative oriented research, a fact that Merton bemoaned: "One gains the impression that focus-group research is being mercilessly misused as quick-and-easy claims for the validity of the research are not subjected to further, quantitative testing" (1987, p. 557).

Criticisms such as these notwithstanding, audience analysis research was and is decidedly interpretive and increasingly dialogic and emancipatory. Its primary goal is to understand the complexities involved in how people understand and interpret media texts. Its methods are almost exclusively qualitative. In contrast to the work of Lazarsfeld and Merton, which focused on expressed content, audience analysis researchers typically focus on group dynamics, believing that the meanings constructed within groups of viewers are largely socially constructed.

For example, Janice Radway used focus groups to great effect in her pioneering research on the reading practices of romance novel enthusiasts that resulted in her 1984 book, *Reading the Romance*. The research took place in and around a local bookstore, and Radway's participants included the storeowner and a group of 42 women who frequented the store and were regular romance readers. Like Morley, Radway developed a mixed-method research design that included text analysis and focus group interviews. Assisted by the bookstore owner (Dot), Radway was able to tap into the activity dynamics of existing networks of women who were avid romance novel readers. These women interacted frequently with Dot about newly published novels, and they interacted with each other as well. Radway simply "formalized" some of these ongoing social activities to generate a systematic and rich store of information about the social circumstances, specific reading practices, attitudes, reading preferences, and multiple and contradictory functions of romance reading among the women she studied. She took her cues about what books to read and what issues to focus discussions around from Dot and her other participants. She read all of the books that her participants read. She talked with many of them informally whenever they were at the bookstore together. And she conducted formal focus groups.

Among other things, Radway noted the importance of group dynamics in how different romance novels were interpreted and used. Even though the novels themselves were read privately, sharing their responses to the novels both in informal conversations and formal focus group discussions was very important to the women. Radway also came to understand how important belonging to a reading group was for mitigating the stigma often associated with the practice of reading romance novels:

> Because I knew beforehand that many women are afraid to admit their preference for romantic novels for fear of being scorned as illiterate or immoral, I suspected that the strength of numbers might make my informants less reluctant about discussing their obsession.
>
> (Radway, 1984, p. 252)

Finally, the ways in which Radway positioned herself within the reading groups was crucial. She noted, for example, that when she was gently encouraging and when she backgrounded her own involvement, "the conversation flowed more naturally as the participants disagreed among themselves, contradicted one another, and delightedly discovered that they still agreed about many things" (p. 48).

All of the various strategies that Radway deployed helped to mobilize the collective energy of the group and to generate kinds and amounts of data that are often difficult, if not impossible, to generate through individual interviews and even observations. Additionally, these strategies—and participation in the focus groups themselves—helped to build a stronger and more effective collective with at least local political teeth. Radway concluded her book-length treatment of her romance novel project with a hopeful yet unfinalized call to praxis, noting that "it is absolutely essential that we who are committed to social change learn not to overlook this minimal but nonetheless legitimate form of protest . . . and to learn how best to encourage it and bring it to fruition" (p. 222)

If the work of Radway began to outline the political, ethical, and praxis potentials of focus groups within qualitative inquiry, the work of Patti Lather attempted to push the "limit conditions" of such work even further. In their book, *Troubling the Angels*, for example, Lather and Smithies (1997) explored the lives, experiences, and narratives of 25 women living with HIV/AIDS. The book is filled with overlapping and contradictory voices that grew out of five years of focus group interviews conducted within different "support groups" in five major cities in Ohio. Lather and Smithies met and talked with their women participants at birthday parties and holiday get-togethers, hospital rooms and funerals, baby showers and picnics. Group dynamics among these women were unpredictable, emotionally charged (even ravaging), and changed constantly across the project. In what she calls a "postbook," Lather (2001, p. 210) acknowledged experiencing at least two "breakdowns" as she bore witness to the women's experiences and stories. Insofar as "breakdowns" are central to human understanding (Heidegger, 1962/1927), clearly these groups were surfaces of/for inquiry and pedagogy for researchers and research participants alike.

In both "strategic" and "found" ways, more organized occasions for "collecting data" constantly blurred into the "practices of everyday life" (deCerteau, 1984). Among other things, this social fact transformed the very nature of the focus groups these researchers conducted, rendering them more like rich and powerful conversations among people who cared deeply for each other. Yet Lather and Smithies were careful to work against the tendency to sentimentalize or roman-ticize their roles or their work by enacting what Lather (2001, p. 212) referred to as a "recalcitrant rhetoric" to counteract tendencies toward *verstehen* or simple empathy. Lather and Smithies tried to remain aware that the goals and rewards of their involvement in the groups were very different from the goals and rewards of their research participants. Their participants, for example, wanted to produce a "K-Mart" book, a collection of autobiographies or autoethnographies of "lived experience." Lather and Smithies were more interested in theorizing their parti-cipants' experiences and foregrounding the political (especially micro-political) dimensions and effects of these experiences. According to Lather, these compet-ing goals were constantly negotiated in focus groups. This pedagogic and politi-cal activity resulted in producing a book that embodies a productive, if uncomfortable/uncomforting, tension between the two competing goals.

Although much of this book is devoted to troubling the waters of ethnographic representation, the experience of conducting fieldwork primarily through focus groups also troubled the waters of research practice. In this regard, Lather and Smithies integrated sociological, political, historical, therapeutic, and pedagogical practices and discourses in their work with the women they studied. In her "postbook," for example, Lather claims to have looked constantly for "the breaks and jagged edges of methodological practices from which we might draw useful knowledge for shaping present practices of a feminist ethnography in excess of our codes but, still: always already forces already active in the present" (2001, pp. 200–201).

One of the most interesting sections of the book for our purposes in this chapter is one in which Lather and Smithies cultivate what they call a "methodology of getting lost":

> At some level, the book is about getting lost across the various layers and registers, about not finding one's way into making a sense that maps easily onto our usual ways of making sense. Here we all get lost: the women, the

> researchers, the readers, the angels, in order to open up present frames of
> knowing to the possibilities of thinking differently.
>
> (Lather and Smithies, 1997, p. 52)

Although these reflections refer to the book itself rather than the process of
conducting the research that led to it, they apply equally well to working with
research participants in the field in the sense that the reflections index the political,
pedagogical, and ethical dimensions of all practices and all knowledge. For
example, Lather and Smithies refused to position themselves as grand theorists
and to interpret or explain the women's lives to them. Instead, they granted

> weight to lived experience and practical consciousness by situating both
> researcher and researched as bearers of knowledge while simultaneously
> attending to the 'price' we pay for speaking out of discourses of truth, forms
> of rationality, effects of knowledge, and relations of power.
>
> (Lather, 2001, p. 215)

Through their tactical positioning, Lather and Smithies both challenged the
researcher's right to know and interpret the experiences of others while they also
interrupted and got in the way of their participants' attempts to narrate their lives
through a kind of innocent ethnographic realism where their voices simply spoke
for themselves in some way (e.g. reading AIDS as the work of God's will).
Additionally, Lather and Smithies acknowledged their impositions and admitted
that a different kind of book—a K-Mart book—might have pleased their participants more. But such a book would have taken Lather and Smithies outside their
own predilections and perhaps competencies as researchers, and is thus a task easier
stated than accomplished. A K-Mart book has never been written, and Lather's
follow-up to *Troubling the Angels* (*Getting Lost*, 2007) is even more theoretical
than the original volume, highlighting the difficulties of accomplishing multiple
interpretive tasks and embodying multiple voices simultaneously.

The various relational and rhetorical tactics enacted by Lather and Smithies
bring to light the very complicated and sometimes troubling micro-politics that
are part and parcel of research practice today (Denzin and Lincoln, 2005, 2011)—
whether or not we are willing to see and enact these micro-politics in our own
work. Lather and Smithies remind us constantly that there are no easy separations
between "researcher" and "researched," that research itself is always already
relational, political, pedagogical, and ethical work, and that we have no alibis for
thinking and acting otherwise. There is no privileged place from which to
experience and to report on experiences objectively—only positions in dialogue.
More than most other research of which we are aware, Lather and Smithies' work
offers us ways to think about research that transcends and transforms the potentials
of using focus groups for re-visioning epistemology, interrogating the relative
purchase of both lived experience and theory, re-imagining ethics within research
practice, and enacting field work in ways that are more attuned to its spiritual,

even sacred, dimensions. And perhaps even more than this, the weaknesses and limitations of Lather and Smithies' work index the many experiential, episte-mological, ethical, theoretical, and all-too-human challenges we still face in conducting qualitative inquiry today (Denzin and Lincoln, 2011). In this regard, focus groups surface the dialogic possibilities inherent in but often thwarted both in everyday social life and in research practice.

What happens in focus groups can help researchers work against premature consolidation of their understandings and explanations thus signaling the limits of reflexivity and the importance of intellectual/empirical modesty as forms of ethics and praxis. Such modesty can allow researchers to engage at least partially in "doubled practices" where we *both* listen to the attempts of others as they make sense of their lives *and* also resist the seductive qualities of "too easy" constructs such as "voice" or "faith" by recognizing and showing how experience itself (as well as our accounts of it) are always constituted within one or another "grand narrative" (Lather, 2001, p. 218). No less than life itself, doing social science has no guarantees.

Conclusions

Focus group work has a long and chaotic history in various domains of applied work. Here, we have tried to offer another kind of approach—one of overlapping genealogies. Using the metaphor of the prism as an organizing trope, we narrated the trajectories of three related functional surfaces of focus group research—the pedagogical, the political, and the empirical. Each of these "surfaces" allows us to mine the unique potentials of focus group conversations. Each gives us a sense of how focus group work offers insights into the ways these groups allow researchers to approach empirical problems in new and creative ways, as well as how they help us generate both understandings and "effectivities" that other research strategies usually do not. Finally, hopefully our accounts of these three functional trajectories of focus group work showed how each primary function is unique and foregrounds certain potentials of focus group work and that all functions are almost always co-present and co-constitutive in most research projects. The pedagogical surface of focus groups highlights the deeply dialogic and transformative nature of such work while showing us that such work has no guarantees. The political surface shows us focus groups as deep sources of collective support around important social issues while alerting us to the dangers of naïve notions of collectivity. The empirical surface highlights the ways inquiry can open deep philosophical questions about the nature of "the research act" itself, including the complex relationship between "self" and "other." Each of these surfaces provides unique insights about how we (and our research participants) can benefit from the legacy of focus group research. Each also offers a partially unique set of ideas, strategies, and practices than can be brought to bear on research today across a variety of domains.

Chapter 3

Key affordances of focus group research

In Chapter 2 we noted that focus group work seems inevitably to involve three primary functions: inquiry, pedagogy, and political effectivity. We also unpacked each of these functions in considerable detail. Although the meanings of each function of focus groups may seem self-explanatory, we would like to reiterate our working definitions of them here. The pedagogic function basically involves collective engagement designed to promote dialogue and achieve higher levels of understanding of issues critical to the development of a group's interests and/or the transformation of conditions of its existence. It is a matter of "reading the word" to better read the world (Freire, 1993/1970). This means asking and answering questions such as the following: What social facts are portrayed in a message as if they were perfectly "natural" or "normal"? Whose positions, interests, and values are represented in the message, and whose are absent or silent? Are any positions, interests, or values ridiculed, vilified, or demonized? How is the message trying to position its readers/viewers? How does this message do its work through the use of specific textual features and specific arrangements of them?

Although not necessarily, the political function of focus group work often builds upon the pedagogic function. The primary goal of the political function is to transform the conditions of existence for particular stakeholders. Activism can grow out of a wide variety of political orientations and typically constitutes a response to conditions of marginalization or oppression. The goal of the political function is usually to transform these conditions, making them more democratic. This may be enacted in a variety of ways including: consciousness raising activities; writing editorials or manifestos, participating in campaigns, public marches, or strikes; boycotting products or services; lobbying government agencies; or simply changing one's lifestyle. In an interview (Kreisler, 2002), linguist and political activist Noam Chomsky cited several key moments of political activism in history that he argues literally changed the world: the Lowell factory girls' protest in the 1850s that catalyzed the US labor movement; the 1960s anti-war, civil rights, and feminist movements; and the efforts of journalists, artists, and public intellectuals in Turkey fighting censorship today through acts of civil disobedience in their everyday professional work. Less obvious, more local forms of activism are also regularly evident everywhere—in neighborhoods, schools, and workplaces. Indexing both the nature and importance of the political function, Chomsky noted that all effective political accomplishments

> got there by struggle, common struggle by people who dedicated themselves with others, because you can't do it alone, and made [this] a much more civilized country. It was a long way to go, and that's not the first time it happened. And it will continue.
>
> (Kreisler, 2002)

Research/Inquiry is perhaps the function most typically associated with focus group research. Yet, it is a slippery term with a long, contested history. At least since the Enlightenment, inquiry has been associated with the so-called hard sciences. From this perspective, reality and knowledge are a priori givens. The primary goals of inquiry have been to explain, predict, and control both natural and social phenomena. Since the "interpretive turn," the nature and scope of inquiry have expanded considerably, with reality considered to be (at least partially) socially constructed and thus changing and changeable. Knowledge is seen as partial and perspectival. The primary goal of inquiry within this view has been to achieve richer, thicker, and more complex levels of understanding. Recently, inquiry has been shown to be messy, dirty, thoroughly imbricated within colonial and neo-colonial impulses, and in need of re-tooling from the ground up to be more praxis-oriented and democratizing (Denzin and Lincoln, 2005, 2011). Based on the emergence of focus group research as a way to answer how and why questions that remained unanswered by positivistic quantitative methods, our working definition of the inquiry function is most closely aligned with that of the "interpretive turn," especially the Chicago School of Sociology. The primary goal of inquiry from this perspective is to generate rich, complex, nuanced, and even contradictory accounts of how people ascribe meaning to and interpret their lived experience with an eye toward how these accounts might be used to affect social policy and change.

Clearly, the boundaries between and among inquiry, pedagogy, and politics within focus group work are porous. Within any given project, these different dimensions/functions of focus group work emerge and interact in distinct, sometimes disjunctive, and often very productive (in Foucault's 1979 sense of producing something new) ways. A discussion of the performative idiom in contemporary qualitative inquiry is useful in understanding how this happens in actual practice. It is to such a discussion that we now turn.

Focus groups and/in the performative turn

Kenneth and Mary Gergen (2012) highlighted three important ways we can think about performative social science. First, they noted that social science research is performed for others. All social science, in one way or another, is concerned with communicating ideas to others. Taking this seriously means thinking about the overlap between the kinds of questions performing artists and social scientists ask—questions about intent, audience, effect, etc. Second, they emphasized the performative nature of language. Echoing J. L. Austin, they noted that language is never simply about communicating information. It is also about expressing, sustaining, and extending relations. Like Austin, they advocated thinking through the effects of our work in the human sciences. What kinds of relationships are conjured up? What are the intended and unintended effects of our work with others? Third, they claimed that performance itself "expands our scope and sensitivities as social scientists." Performance highlights the aesthetics of attending to the world and reporting upon it for others. Performance gives us no recourse to objectivity (Gergen and Gergen, 2012, pp. 11–12).

We look to extend this discussion here. Long connected with theater and elocution, performance has more recently emerged as a basic, ontological but inherently contested concept "because when we understand performance beyond theatrics and recognize it as fundamental and inherent to life and culture we are confronted with the ambiguities of different spaces and places that are foreign, contentious, and often under siege" (Madison and Hamera, 2006, p. xii). Across the academy, this turn to performance has posed new questions about our understandings of texts, practices, identities, and cultures, allowing us to see the world as perpetually in motion. Such a notion of performance gives us nowhere to hide in our responsibilities for the work we do, forcing us to see the routine as potentially ambiguous, foreign, and contentious.

The performative turn has opened up powerful spaces for thinking about emergent methodologies that "explore new ways of thinking about and framing knowledge construction," remaining ever-conscious of the links among epistemologies, methodologies, and the techniques used to carry out empirical work (Hesse-Biber and Leavy, 2006, pp. xi–xii). From this perspective, inquiry (especially qualitative inquiry) is no longer a discrete set of methods we deploy functionally to solve problems defined a priori. Instead, we must question the reification of particular methods that has marked the emergence of qualitative inquiry as a trans-disciplinary field (Kamberelis and Dimitriadis, 2005).

Because the performative turn has de-centered the research act—opening up spaces that de facto collapse demarcations between and among research, pedagogy, and activism—re-imagining qualitative inquiry largely involves seeing it more as a matter of asking and dwelling in new questions that are not definitively answerable. Although we look to open discussion about the ways different strategies and practices can coalesce productively and synergistically, we do not advocate an "anything goes" position. The competencies required by each dimension of focus group work demands specific skills that are not readily transferred from one dimension to another.

Our orientation to focus group work encourages a new angle of vision on the politics of evidence. Mindful of the best impulses of the sociology of knowledge and the attendant co-implication of knowledge and power, the new politics of evidence, we believe, must attend to the specificity and autonomy of evidence in new ways. Recognizing that evidence never "speaks for itself," a key task today is finding ways to use evidence to challenge our thoughts and practices. By locating focus groups within a performative idiom and at the intersection of research, pedagogy, and politics, we are provided no "alibis" for our work. For example, we cannot attend to the political dimension of our work without also considering the traditional empirical dimensions. And we cannot attend to either without also considering the ways our work circulates pedagogically. As we argued in Chapter 2, focus group work is thus inevitably prismatic, with all three faces of the prism visible to some extent no matter which face we fix on or how we direct our gaze. In sum, a broader conception of focus group work that attends to its wide range of quasi-unique affordances is useful for thinking about the myriad potentials— both discovered and not-yet imagined—for human science research.

Quasi-unique affordances of focus group research

All strategies for gathering information from research participants have different affordances—that is, they are likely to allow researchers to learn some things and not others or some things more than others. For example, some kinds of information (especially how people engage in common practices) reveal themselves in the context of their everyday lives—in the situated activities or practices that constitute their personal or professional lives, in their recreational activities, or in their everyday attempts to negotiate power or to get things done. Extensive observations in the context of a naturalistic study are particularly useful for capturing and understanding these activities and practices. Other kinds of information are more likely to reveal themselves in more contrived research contexts such as quasi-experiments or experiments where researchers create situations for people to demonstrate skills and knowledges that they might not reveal if we just waited for them to occur spontaneously, as in naturalistic studies. If we wanted to learn about the most effective way to become competent at a particular skill or practice (or the various ways people learn a particular skill or practice), for example, we might want to create a number of different situations in which this kind of learning might happen, engage different research participants in these various situations, and analyze the similarities and differences in the kinds and amounts of learning that occurred in each of them. Still other kinds of information are most readily accessed by engaging individuals in conversational interviews about experiences or issues that really matter to them in their lives. In this regard, coming to understand the experiences of grief or personal tragedy is often most successfully accomplished by conducting one-on-one conversational interviews that "pull for" stories of experience and reflections upon those stories. Finally, to understand research participants' durable dispositions and orientations to social activities or issues (as well as how these dispositions became sedimented over time), conducting one-on-one life-history interviews is a particularly effective strategy. These kinds of interviews allow researchers to tap what Bourdieu (1990) calls *habitus* and Gee (2011) calls *primary discourses*, which are the sedimented ways of thinking, feeling, believing, and acting that we develop during our early socialization experiences and that continue to exert powerful effects on our behaviors, beliefs, ideologies, and practices throughout our lives.

Focus groups have some quasi-unique affordances compared to other data collection strategies. It is not so much that they allow researchers to gather certain kinds of information that could not be gathered using other strategies; it is more that they are likely to allow researchers to generate more focused, richer, more complex, and more nuanced information, especially in relation to certain topics or domains of inquiry. With savvy, responsive facilitation, focus groups can draw out several information gathering affordances in especially powerful ways.

Some of the most important and powerful affordances of focus group work we have gleaned from the research literature and our own research include the following:

- Focus groups can (and often do) mitigate or inhibit the authority of the researcher, allowing participants to "take over" or "own" the interview space, which usually results in richer, deeper understandings of whatever is being studied.
- The leveling of power relations between researchers and research participants usually also allows researchers to explore group dynamics, the lifeblood of social activity, as well as to explore the constitutive power of discourse in people's lives.
- Although not entirely "naturalistic," focus groups can afford a closer approximation to natural interaction than do individual interviews.
- Focus groups are particularly useful for filling in gaps in understandings derived primarily from observations, especially the *hows* and *whys* behind things observed or mentioned in casual interactions.
- Another affordance of focus group research is to draw out complexities, nuances, and contradictions with respect to whatever is being studied. The intensely social nature of focus groups tends to promote a kind of "memory synergy" among participants, and it can motivate efforts to bring forth the "collective memory" of particular social groups or formations (e.g. African Americans, wounded war veterans, former cult members). Because they emerge as a confluence of varied perspectives on similar experiences, focus groups often surface eclipsed or invisible connections between and among constitutive social, cultural, and political structures and forces. In other words, they are effective tools for making the invisible visible.
- Finally, focus groups can (and often do) become democratic spaces for solidarity building and political effectivity—promoting political synergy among participants, which often leads to concrete and effective social or political activist work.

In the remainder of this chapter, we unpack each of these affordances in greater detail and provide examples from the research literature of some of the ways they have played out in actual practice.

Mitigating researchers' authority and generating deeper understandings

Focus groups can mitigate or inhibit the authority of the researcher, allowing participants to "take over" or "own" the interview space, which can result in richer, deeper understandings of whatever is being studied. As noted above, the so-called "performative turn" in qualitative methodology has posed new challenges for how we answer for our research—our work in the field and the work at our desks. A key challenge here is working against premature closure in our understanding of the world, to avoid succumbing to the temptations of weak evidence. Focus groups offer the researcher unique opportunities to diminish the authority and control that can lead to premature closure and weak standards of evidence. Of course, they do not do this necessarily or automatically. But with skillful, responsive, empathic facilitation, focus groups can go a long way toward democratizing interactional spaces, allowing participants a sense of safety and ownership of the activity, and thus increasing the likelihood of generating deep, rich, complex understandings of the issues under study.

We thus see "mitigating authority" and "generating deeper understandings" as twinned phenomena. Several studies have demonstrated the power of mitigating the researcher's authority in focus groups. We highlight one such example here— Marc Lamont Hill's *Beats, Rhymes, and Classroom Life* (2009). We chose this study because it offers an example of group discussions that draw on the affordances of focus groups without being marked as such. In this study Hill developed a "Hip Hop Lit" class in a relatively poor, urban Philadelphia high school, along with a teacher at the school, Mr. Columbo. Although he was not officially a teacher at the time, Hill developed the curricula and implemented it over the course of a school year as part of an afterschool program called "The Twilight Program." The class was divided up into several modules including Roots of Hip Hop and Literature, Love, Family, The Hood, Politics, and Despair. The class consisted of largely (though not exclusively) African American students. Both Hill and Columbo were relatively young when they did this work. Hill is African American; Columbo is white.

Hill did not call the discussion sessions that happened in the class "focus groups." However, they clearly bore a strong family resemblance to what we have described as focus groups throughout this book. Recall that one of our goals here is to push the boundaries of how focus groups have been conceptualized and used—to imagine the entire landscape of focus group form and function. To do this requires seeking out examples of facilitated group discussions even if such discussions were not explicitly marked as focus groups by their authors. The discussion groups conducted by Hill and Colombo represent a really good example of studies that help us push both conceptual and pragmatic understandings of the potentials of focus group work.

Across several of the chapters in *Beats, Rhymes, and Classroom Life*, Hill documented the ways he discussed complex personal and social issues with his students through the lens of hip hop. These included, for example, the ways notions of "the real" are negotiated and contested in hip hop. According to Hill, the notion of "the real" itself was contested in the group—pulled between "The Heads" who located it in a deep and elitist knowledge of hip hop and others who located it in "the streets." Hill explained the contestation over "the real" and its "performances" in ways that really show how mitigating authority often leads to deeper levels of understanding.

In an early discussion of hip hop and "the real with his students," Hill came face-to-face with some of his own presuppositions about hip hop. He realized, for example, that the texts he had chosen for discussion were often closest in spirit and content to the elitist taste of "the Heads."

> My choices were reflective of a broader tendency within my HHBE [Hip Hop Based Education] contexts documented in the research literature. Typically, HHBE educators choose texts that they deem politically, intellectually, or culturally sophisticated or relevant. While appropriate, such moves often lead to the development of curricula that respond to the interests, experiences, and generational orientation of the teacher rather than the student.
>
> (Hill, 2009, p. 39)

Hill's insights about the need to back away from his own interests and preferences was largely afforded by the "performative" space he and Mr. Columbo constituted with these youth—a space where notion of "hip hop" itself was open to contestation.

In his chapter on "wounded healers," we see the mitigation of Hill's authority most clearly. Here, Hill reflected upon the community space as one where youth can be vulnerable in sharing their stories. Although there was initially some reluctance to share personal stories with the group, this changed quite dramatically when one young woman named Robin made a personal disclosure while discussing rapper Lauren Hill's song "Manifest," about a bad relationship. This led to a discussion about how the students were uncomfortable being the first person to talk about a new issue or topic. One girl named Dorene said, "I remember Robin said something about love and it was deep and then everybody wanted so start saying stuff." Two girls responded "Exactly!" and "True!" before Lisa said, "When Robin started talking I felt like I could say whatever I had to say" (p. 67). Importantly, Hill (Marc) made himself vulnerable during these discussions as well.

During a discussion of fatherhood, for example, Hill revealed that he was soon going to be the father of a daughter: "I have a baby on the way right now that I didn't expect. Her mom is six months pregnant, and I'm really stressin' about it. I ain't worried about money or nothin' like that. It's just . . . I wasn't expecting this, and she and I not together and she [the mother] gotta be in my life forever" (p. 86). The students "co signed" (to use Hill's term) his experiences, and a discussion started about the role of parenting and gender roles. Some of the students had had similar experiences and shared them: "I feel you. My baby moms be trippin'" (p. 86). Hill made himself "vulnerable" here and opened a safe space for his participants.

Interestingly, part of becoming vulnerable and mitigating his authority required that Hill negotiate a particular kind of role in the classroom—a role different from Mr. Columbo who was a formal teacher in the school. Their very different roles positioned them in relation to the students in very different ways and with different effects. Because of his official role as teacher, Mr. Columbo did not "self disclose." The group noticed this and discussed why Mr. Columbo was so reticent in discussions, providing both racial and status explanations for his behavior. One young man commented, "He just, y'ah mean, he can't relate 'cause he from, you know, a different culture so he don't want to say nothin'." A young woman responded, "Other people can't relate too but they try . . . And he a *teacher*" (p. 89). This young woman highlighted the different roles of the facilitators in the group—the white teacher and the African American researcher and how they were able to take up personal issues differently or constrained in taking up some roles at all. Although Hill and Columbo worked out their roles in the classroom in different ways, each was aware of how mitigating and negotiating their authority made a difference in the work they did. Their insights and reflections in this regard were "read back" by the students and opened up for discussion. In the democratized interactional space of their classroom, students were increasingly willing to share personal issues, which, among other things, yielded data that were very rich indeed.

In sum, focus groups always allow for the negotiation of one's presence in the field. For Hill, he came to understand the ways hip hop can serve as a space for storytelling, rooted in "wounded healing." In being reflective about the circulation of authority and control, Hill cultivated a space of mutual vulnerability, a space that allowed these young people new ways to connect to hip hop texts with which they were very familiar, to each other, and to Hill. In turn, this allowed Hill to explore hip hop in new ways—ways inspired issues and themes that mattered deeply to his students—generational identity, "realness," and the power of collective remembering. Key here was how Hill's work was enabled by the affordances of focus groups, especially the ability to negotiate one's role in relation to authority and power relations.

Disclosing the constitutive power of discourse and the lifeblood of social activity

The leveling of power relations between researchers and research participants usually also allows researchers to witness something close to "natural" group dynamics. In this witnessing, the power of discourse in people's lives and how discourse constitutes the lifeblood of social activity are revealed. At least since the

Chicago School of Sociology emerged in the early part of the twentieth century, the constitutive power of talk in the development and maintenance of all forms of communal life has been widely acknowledged and exploited within the interpretive research community. The Chicago School included many of the twentieth century's most brilliant sociologists and social theorists including Robert Park, Ernest Burgess, William Foote Whyte, and Frederic Thrasher. All were devoted to understanding the complexities of contemporary urban life, especially in relation to immigration issues. Many Chicago School scholars were interested in understanding how "natural areas" such as the Jewish ghetto (Wirth, 1928), hobo jungles (Anderson, 1923), and areas that housed gangs (Thrasher, 1927) came to be. All grounded their work in the everyday lives of the people they studied, and all found that patterns of talk and social interaction were central to what one might call the lifeblood of the social formations or communities in which their participants lived and worked. For example, William Foote Whyte's classic *Street Corner Society: The Social Structure of an Italian Slum* (1993/1943) is a descriptive account of "Cornerville" (a pseudonym for Boston's North End). The book tells the story of two men—the resistant "Doc" and the assimilationist "Chick," two different examples of how Italian immigrant groups dealt with life in America. Whyte emphasized throughout that much of what happened in the process of researching and writing this book took place in a kind of ad hoc fashion. His research was a profoundly human endeavor, taking place at the intersection of different individuals with different social needs, agendas, and goals, all in an intensely local and particular context. He also emphasized that "the researcher, like his informants, is a social animal," and he argues that a "real explanation . . . necessarily involves a rather personal account of how the researcher lived during the period of study" (p. 279). And, in fact, Whyte provides just such a narrative—complete with contingencies, unexpected events, failures, etc. In short, he demonstrates how his work in "Cornerville" came into being through talk and social interaction in the same way that the community itself came into being and continued to develop.

In *Talk and Social Theory*, Fred Erickson (2004) reminded us of many of the important insights about the constitutive power of talk generated by scholars associated with the Chicago School tradition. More specifically, he demonstrated how everyday talk is fundamentally linked to broader social processes including the constitution and maintenance of social formations, cultures, and social movements. Through the use of telling examples, Erickson illustrated how these linkages are *both* uniquely crafted by particular social actors for accomplishing specific purposes in specific situations, *and* also profoundly informed by and partially constituted by social and cultural processes that extend far beyond specific instances of talk in specific situations. In short, Erickson explored and exposed the mutually reinforcing connections between the local conduct of talk and the general functioning of social formations, institutions, and society itself.

Mitchell Duneier's (1994) *Slim's Table: Race, Respectability, and Masculinity* is a powerful example of the ways in which talk brings communities into being and is responsible for how they remain the same or change over time. Rooted in the ethos and world view of the Chicago School scholars, Duneier studied the lives and stories told by a group of African American (and some white) men who hung out together in a neighborhood eating establishment called "Valois" on the south side of Chicago in the late 1980s and early 1990s. Duneier, too, ate and hung out at Valois, listening to conversations and stories, entering some conversations, and eventually conducting individual and group interviews with some of the cafeteria's "regulars." Importantly, although the conversations that Duneier listened to and participated in were not marked as focus groups per se, their shape and functions were nearly identical to more traditional focus groups, especially once influenced by the "performative turn" wherein facilitators assume a minor role in directing conversation. Indeed, as we have emphasized throughout, exploiting the affordances of focus group work is simultaneously an exploration of its many possible forms and functions.

As we mentioned, although some of the "regulars" showcased in this book were white and/or middle class, most were older black working-class men living in or nearby the neighborhood where Valois was located. Most of these men were single, employed, and living in rooms or small apartments in the neighborhood. As we read accounts of the talk and social interaction that occurred between and among these men at Valois, we are struck by how compassionate, loyal, and morally upright they are. Their self-worth and the worth they see in others derives from upholding personal standards of caring, civility, solidarity, decency, honesty, pride, discretion, and moderation. We are also struck by how their ways of talking and interacting with each other constitute and perpetuate a particular kind of *communitas*. Rooted in the African American cultural tradition of "care" for others in conditions of violence and oppression, the bonds between and among these men (as well as their bonds with friends, family members, and even acquaintances) have been wrought from their commitments to compassion, loyalty, and personal integrity. Their moral compasses are unwavering; their virtues permeate all of their table talk interactions; as they share all of their dreams, hopes, frustrations, and losses with each other, they reveal themselves to be men of extraordinary substance and character at a time when such attributes have become both scarce and undervalued. Were this not the case, they would not remain in the circle of "regulars." Their talk and social interaction would not be sanctioned because it would contaminate the lifeblood of the group.

With respect to our purposes in this chapter, Duneier's work is exemplary for a variety of reasons. Like many other studies we have showcased, it clearly demonstrates the blurry boundaries between what has traditionally been considered focus group work and the wide range of speech events whose forms and functions resemble traditional focus groups, thus allowing us to imagine the boundaries of focus groups in increasingly wider ways. Perhaps more than any other study with which we are familiar, Duneier's work also demonstrates in clear and powerful ways how the lifeblood of any group or community is constituted (both habitually and ritually) through everyday talk and social interaction, as well as how focus groups can be spaces for performing something very close to natural talk and social interaction. Finally, in the spirit of William Foote Whyte's insights about the lineaments of fieldwork, Duneier's discussions of how he entered into conversations at Valois, which paved the way for his research, underscore the fundamental importance of building and sustaining relationships in the research process. Only when one is successful at doing this does one begin to yield data that truly reflect the rich and variegated fabric of social life one is studying. Indeed, Duneier's work at Valois was talked into being in much the same way that the micro-community of "regulars" itself was talked into being and continued to develop. And this fact was crucial to what Duneier learned and the accounts he was able to generate from what he learned.

Approximating the natural

Although not entirely "natural," focus groups can afford a closer approximation to natural interaction than do many other data collection strategies and activities. As noted earlier, our approach to focus group work is rooted in the performative turn in qualitative inquiry. From this perspective the line between focus groups and everyday interaction becomes blurry. That is, if everyday interactions themselves are performances, then focus groups can be ways to invoke and access the very dynamics of these performances. We highlight here another example of research that utilized focus group strategies in complex and expansive ways—The Echoes of Brown Project that Michelle Fine headed up with several students and colleagues. The Echoes of Brown project had its roots in The Educational Opportunity Gap Project (EOGP), which involved scores of youth in documenting and understanding the so-called "achievement gap" from *their* point of view. The project ran from 2001 to 2003 and involved a series of "research camps" where over 100 youth from urban and suburban schools in New York and New Jersey met with researchers from the CUNY Graduate Center to "study youth perspectives on racial and class based (in)justice in schools and the nation" (Torre et al., 2008, p. 28). The participants became familiar with a host of techniques, including developing and administrating surveys, interviewing, and conducting focus groups. Together with these youth, Fine and her colleagues documented finance inequalities between urban and suburban schools, the steady erosion of desegregation policies, the racializing of academic tracking within schools, the profound ways that class, race, and ethnicity affect tracking, statistics related to the disproportionate number of black students to receive suspensions, expulsions and other disciplinary actions (pp. 30–31).

The last issue became something of a rallying point that ended up distinguishing the EOGP from the Brown Project in important ways. Part of the EOGP was to share the data with key stakeholders including school officials. As Fine and others made clear, they first attempted to present research findings to schools as part of "feedback sessions." One young man named Kareem highlighted some of the empirical material he had helped to gather on disproportionate suspension rates among young, African American males. "Now I'd like you to look at the suspension data, and notice that Black males in high school were twice as likely as White males to be suspended, and there are almost no differences between Black males and Black females" (p. 31). The teachers present, however, were resistant to Kareem's presentation despite the fact that "Kareem provided clear evidence that tore at the ideological representation of the school as integrated and fair" (p. 32). The response was defensive and the room "calcified" in defiance.

The team then "decided to move [their] critical scholarship to performance" (p. 32). Working with youth at these same schools, as well as "with community elders, social scientists, spoken word artists, dancers, choreographers, and a video crew" the team explored the data from the EOGP project from the preceding years. They also developed and conducted creative theater workshops to learn more about Brown and to create a performance "that brought together political history, personal experience, research, and knowledge gathered from generations living in the immediate and the long shadow of Brown" (p. 33). The performance took place on May 14, 2004 in front of an audience of 800. In addition, a DVD/book was generated from this work, which included interviews with elders and much of the poetry and performances of the youth (including spoken word pieces and dances). But perhaps most interestingly (for our purposes), the DVD shows how the creative texts and performances of these young people themselves were generated.

For example, there are segments on the DVD that show youth actively engaged in workshop activities with their teachers, and there are segments that chronicle the development of several written texts and dance pieces. Although these workshops were ostensibly led by resident artists and scholars, much of the "pedagogy" that happened within them ended up being dialogic and democratic with the students performing as much teaching as learning. For example, we see one very telling vignette on the DVD where an older spoken word artist was engaging the young people in exercises meant to develop their own pieces. He encouraged them to connect the material to social justice issues they have experienced. One young woman offered the example of "cursing in textbooks." This comment activated the group's collective memory and mobilized the students to share stories of this experience. A carnivalesque dialogue broke out. At one point, the artist in residence seemed confused about the meaning of "cursing in textbooks." Noticing this, the young woman explained that they have old textbooks that often have curse words written in the margins. Others agreed and affirmed the veracity of the claim. One young white woman made a connection between this issue and *Catcher in the Rye*— a place in that novel where the protagonist Holden Caulfield says he can't get any peace anywhere because the word "fuck" is written everywhere. Talk then turned to the age of the textbooks themselves—how older relatives who attended the same school had used the same textbooks. This led to even more trenchant criticisms of quality and equity issues related to school materials, tasks, and practices. This brief account of a single event from an EOGP workshop is illustrative not only of the generativity of these workshops but also of the potentialities of focus group work in general. As such, it reflects some dimensions of the expanded notions of the forms, functions, and affordances of focus groups we are trying to construct in this book, especially with respect to "creating" naturalistic stages for re-performing everyday knowledge and practice.

In the EOGP project, politically powerful spoken word poetry and dance emerged from focus group activities. Invoking insights from the "performative turn" in social science research, Fine and her colleagues shared their acute awareness that data never simply speak for themselves but must always be made visible to audiences in relevant (and often innovative) ways. Invoking the pioneering work of Mary Louise Pratt, Fine referred to her focus group formations as "contact zones," "social spaces where disparate cultures meet, clash, grapple with each other, often in highly asymmetrical relations of power" (Pratt, 1991, quoted in Torre et al., 2008, p. 24). The projects Fine and her colleagues initiated did indeed bring together youth from different class, races, and ethnicities. As one participant noted:

> Participating in something like Echoes and the Arts and Social Justice Institute was the first time where I had to work as closely and as intensely as I did with people who were so different from me. The project brought youth from very different racial, economic, academic, and social backgrounds into one space to be creative and to most importantly just be themselves. The comfort and safety that was established in the very beginning was instrumental in allowing for the work to get done and the performance to be shaped and constructed.
> (Torre et al., 2008, p. 24)

As "contact zones," conversations, focus groups, workshops, performances, and the like are remarkably similar to one another. Thinking about these various speech events as "contact zones" allows us to see broad continuities in both form and function across them. And the insights that emerge from this process allow us to re-conceptualize "the natural" as a diverse set of spaces and practices shot through with potential problems and possibilities. As key elements of the "performative turn" in human science research, focus groups help us rethink the nature of social interaction itself and to trouble received binaries such as natural-contrived and authentic-performed.

Filling in knowledge gaps and saturating understanding

Focus groups are particularly useful for filling in gaps in understandings derived primarily from observations and other methods such as surveys and one-on-one interviews. Although we have been critical of deploying focus groups as sub-ordinate to other forms of data collection strategies (particularly in relation to quantitative data), they do pair nicely with other modes of data collection in certain research contexts. In particular, focus groups can be used strategically to saturate understandings of key issues disclosed in partial or understated ways during the research process. For example, Getnet Tizazu Fetene of Addis Ababa University in Ethiopia used focus groups to understand how young college students understood HIV/AIDS (see Fetene, 2009). As Getnet found, the source of the problem of HIV/AIDS in Ethiopia has been constructed primarily as a kind of "knowledge gap" (see Fetene and Dimitriadis, 2010, for a more in-depth discussion of this issue). For example, a government report framed the problem as one of understanding preventative measurements—the more, the better.

> Measuring comprehensive knowledge of the respondents by taking those who knew all three preventive methods and with no misconceptions was found to be low (less than 20 percent), which is in agreement with UNAIDS reports. Comprehensive knowledge seems to increase along with increase in educational level.
>
> (Ministry of Health, 2004, p. 38)

Getnet wanted to understand the phenomena in more depth. In addition to administering a survey, he deployed several qualitative data collection strategies, including ethnographic observation and document analysis. He also attempted to conduct one-on-one interviews but had little success. Focus groups turned out to be the best method for understanding young people's contemporary mores, beliefs and practices related to HIV/AIDS in Ethiopia. With the assistance of a co-researcher, he conducted focus groups with ten young men and ten young women. Several new and provocative findings emerged from these groups related to contemporary understandings of HIV/AIDS; new attitudes towards sex and relationships; and condom use.

Many of Getnet's participants reported that they were weary of being inundated with information about HIV/AIDS and that such information no longer had any educational or preventative effectivity:

KALEB: HIV/AIDS is a subject that I have known since I was a kid. Let alone talking about it with my friends seriously, I don't even want it to be mentioned. I think this is the overall feeling here. Suppose one announces to talk about HIV even at a time when there are no exams, in a situation where students have nothing serious to do, nobody would bother to attend the talk. On the contrary, we would say, "What the hell is he talking about? If he wishes, let me give him a lecture on it! *Sira fetual*? ['Doesn't he have anything to do?'] Students feel they know every thing about AIDS.

MINYICHEL: He [Kaleb] is right. The subject of AIDS has become boring. If one says let us talk about AIDS, every one would say, "Fuck you!"

In addition, Getnet found that new mores around sex and sexuality have emerged with many youth reporting that romantic relationships are beginning at younger and younger ages.

GETNET: *How common is it to have boyfriends and girlfriends among college students here?*

ELIAS: It is very common. It is even observable among elementary school students. Even though I don't want to talk about a figure I don't have at hand with a note of certainty, I'd say over 80% of college students have got boyfriends/ girlfriends.

GETNET: *That is interesting. What do you say on this, guys? Minyichel?*

MINYICHEL: This is a reality. I mean it is a fact. . . In the past, we heard stories that university was a place for university students to engage to one another and become future partners, I mean husbands and wives. But nowadays the thing is like a game. I mean having boyfriends and girlfriends at university level.

GETNET: *Some kind of routine?*

MINYICHEL: Yeah. You know, it [the practice] is there. But there is nothing genuine about it. There is nothing right!

GETNET: *I see! Ok, Kaleb. Go ahead!*

KALEB: More or less my brothers have said it. What I want to add is a little more. I mean, this is a reality! Let alone in this university, students are having [boyfriends and girlfriends] at lower levels including the preparatory level. As my brother said, the figure would be 80 to 85%. If there are students without friends, it is because of fear of HIV/AIDS, or because of something or family members or lack of "business" [the financial resources]. Or someone who believes he doesn't have "business."

Despite this trend of young people having sex earlier and earlier, there are longstanding conservative attitudes about sex and sexuality that make purchasing condoms difficult. Several of the young men and women reported that they are still embarrassed by purchasing condoms. In addition, romantic relationships are still riddled with patriarchal notions and power dynamics and where men are very much still in control.

SARA: I also feel they [guys] are disgusted with it. Because guys don't have fear of pregnancy, they don't want to use condoms for preventing pregnancy. They might worry about catching AIDS, but when they are in the heat of the moment, they don't want to think of using condoms. They think that they wouldn't get the satisfaction they need if they use condoms.

ADEY: I'd like to say more on this feeling of disgust with condom use. Guys usually say they lose their sensations. Their feelings become dead when they have to use condoms. They say it does not give them any satisfaction when they use condoms.

MELAT: Yeah, that's true. Guys are often heard saying sex with condom is like licking Desta Candy [a very popular locally produced candy] with its wrap on.

As Getnet demonstrated, the young people in his study were facing something like a perfect storm. They were saturated with information about HIV/AIDS;

longstanding mores around sex and sexuality are changing; yet puritanical and patriarchal ideologies about sex prevail. All these social factors help to explain why knowledge about condoms and condom use does not always translate into practice.

In form at least, Getnet's focus groups were probably the most prototypic kinds of focus groups we have discussed in this chapter. Like the less prototypic kinds we have discussed, however, they were extremely effective at surfacing kinds of information that would have less likely surfaced using other data collection strategies. Recall, for example, that his participants did not respond well to discussing sensitive topics related to sex and HIV/AIDS in one-on-one interviews. In fact, their unresponsiveness was a primary reason why he depended so heavily on focus groups to collect his data, and they proved to be invaluable for saturating his understandings of the many complex material and ideological forces that accounted for young people's sexual practices and their relations to HIV/AIDS. Indeed, when the authority of the researcher was diluted and the discussions were "owned" by groups of peers, participants were both comfortable and forth-coming about sharing the abundance of information they had related to major social problems. Importantly, much of this information challenged status quo beliefs about childhood and adolescence, sex, condom use, and HIV/AIDS. We will return to this study later in discussing other affordances of focus group work.

Drawing out complexity, nuance, and contradiction

Another affordance of focus group research is to draw out complexities, nuances, and contradictions with respect to whatever is being studied. The intensely social nature of focus group work often elicits subtexts and cognitive and emotional "breakdowns," which, among other things, index sensitive issues and problems that research participants may have alluded to but have not addressed directly. This "tip of the iceberg" character of focus group work is especially useful for reminding researchers to work against premature consolidations of their understandings and explanations, thus signaling the limits of reflexivity.

Focus groups were used effectively to draw out complexity, nuance, and contradiction in Michelle Fine and Lois Weis's work with poor and working-class young adults in Buffalo, New York and Jersey City, New Jersey. This work resulted in *The Unknown City* (1998) and other publications (e.g. Weis, 2004). Fine and Weis conducted interviews and focus groups with African American, Caucasian, and Puerto Rican men and women around issues of domestic abuse, the police, and schooling experiences. *The Unknown City* presents a kaleidoscopic view of how the general loss of public safety nets was understood differently by different groups. For example, Caucasian men tended not to implicate larger structural forces in explaining their social and economic circumstances. In contrast, African American men provided sophisticated structural explanations for their circum-stances, including the role of the police in their neighborhoods.

Additionally, Caucasian women had different perspectives than African American women on many social issues. Their understandings and explanations of domestic violence were particularly telling in this regard. Both African American women and Caucasian women discussed domestic violence. Discussions of domestic violence were more frequent among Caucasian women. Yet these women were reluctant to name white men as perpetrators, typically locating cause elsewhere (Weis, 2004, p. 41). In contrast, African American women held black men responsible for violence in the homes. Weis noted, "It is striking that White women are reluctant to name domestic violence as a problem in the community, although obviously it is, whereas Black women speak openly and directly about violence in their homes" (Weis, 2004, p. 41).

The role of focus groups was crucial for unpacking these differences and the reasons behind them. In general, Caucasian women were more reluctant than African American women to speak publically about their experiences. They voiced them privately in one-on-one settings. Additionally, Caucasian women tended to understand and explain their experiences in highly personal, psychological terms— as secrets not to be shared with others (or at least not many others). They did not like to discuss them in focus groups. They shared "rarely," and:

> the intimacies shared in an interview about individual men [did] not translate into collective sharing, nor [did] they spur a critical analysis of the role of family, heterosexuality, and/or men in ways that begin to break the patterns of violence that regulate gender relations inside some poor and working-class White families.
>
> (Weis, 2004, p. 45)

For the Caucasian women, there was a clear disjuncture between the individual interviews and the focus groups. In the former, abuse was shared as an individual, private problem. In the latter, abuse was avoided as a whole.

In contrast, in both individual interviews and focus groups, African American women tended to talk more publicly, and their stories included more structural, sociological explanations.

> Unlike White women, African American women spoke in focus group as well as in individual interviews, where they shared experiences of pain and suffering as well as strength and hope. They [told] and [retold] stories of abuse to one another, with sympathetic nods all around.
>
> (Weis, 2004, p. 45)

In this regard, Weis discussed one such group where a woman shared a story of abuse that also implicated the involvement of and the limits of police and other official state entities. She narrated how the police were called by relatives, how restraining orders were issued, and how court dates were delayed, etc.; all to very little avail. One woman named Ayisha said,

If you do something to protect your own self, you get in more trouble with the law. It's easier for you to take actions into your own hand [than trust the cops and/or courts], but then you're in trouble with the law. And to me it causes too many problems for the law to be able to take care of it. You have to go through so much. You have to get a restraining order. You have to go through being put on the calendar in the court system. You have to go through trials, where this person might show up and that person might not show up.

(Weis, 2004, p. 47)

As Ayisha unfolded her argument, "the women [were] shaking their heads in strong agreement" (p. 47).

More generally, Weis found that domestic violence is more likely to spill out into the public domain in African American communities than in white ones. Documenting the experiences of a woman named Ayisha, Weis reported that "[w]hile the original incident involved a woman and her boyfriend, it quickly involved a large number of people: her mother, the boyfriend's mother and son, her sisters, brother, and an aunt. This all took place within less than an hour" (p. 48). Domestic abuse was experienced publically and addressed publically. Coming to understand both the experiences of domestic violence among African American women and white women, as well as how these different groups of women were willing (or not willing) to share their experiences in different social contexts, happened largely as a function of the focus group component of Fine and Weis's work. Their focus groups became key public sites where complexities, nuances, and contradictions related to ostensibly similar experiences that were taken up very differently by different groups of people could be brought to light. More specifically, focus groups were crucial for understanding some of the complexities, nuances, and contradictions of the experience of domestic violence within and across racial lines. They were also crucial for understanding the ways that men of different races understood and explained the reasons for their social and economic circumstances. In the most general sense, the focus groups in this study became staging grounds for understanding how race, class, gender, and their various intersections contribute to how social phenomena such as poverty and domestic violence are experienced, understood, and explained in different ways for different groups. Indeed, the focus groups brought into high relief various disjunctures in the lives and practices of white and African American men and women with respect to a host of social issues. For the African American women, the intensely social nature of focus groups also tended to promote a kind of "collective remembering" (e.g. Wertsch, 2002) among participants that allowed them to make connections between their own personal experiences in the present with histories of oppression with respect to the social and economic structures and forces that undergird both. One participant's story of experience will remind other participants of related experiences, which they want to share, in a kind of chain reaction of storytelling ensues. These are, again, unique affordances of focus groups.

Disclosing eclipsed or invisible connections

We use the somewhat unusual term *disclosing* intentionally here. It is a term coined by Martin Heidegger (e.g. 1962/1927, 1971, 1993) to talk about how we engage in genuine modes of being and saying to "bring forth" the essence or organization of all things and their contexts. Such disclosing activity has become particularly relevant in the complexly connected, globalized environments where most of us now conduct research. Responding to this social fact, George Marcus's (1998) insights about postmodern, multi-sited ethnographies are especially relevant here. In postmodern, multi-sited ethnographies, relevant comparative dimensions develop as a function of the fractured, discontinuous plane of movement and discovery among sites. As the researcher maps an object of study, she often finds herself needing to posit logics of relationship, translation, and association among several real or virtual sites. She must attend to comparisons that arise from putting questions to an emergent domain of inquiry or object of study whose lineaments are not known beforehand. She recognizes that most objects of study are mobile and multiply situated. She draws lines of connection in the process of research that have previously been thought to be (or have been conceptually kept) "worlds apart." There is, then, an inherent metaphoric character to the research process. The global is collapsed into and made an integral part of parallel, related local situations and flows (of culture, ethnicities, economic capital, etc.—see Appadurai, 1990). Interpretive accounts are thus created in a landscape for which there is yet a map—an "accepted" theoretical or descriptive model. Researchers and their participants contribute to shaping the objects they study in the absence of reliable models of macro-processes for contextualizing referents of research such as "the world system," "capitalism," "the state," "the nation," etc.

In many ways, focus group work often involves and integrates Heidegger's disclosing activity and Marcus's postmodern ethnographic strategies in powerful though often tacit ways. Emily Martin's (1995) work, which is reported in a book titled *Flexible Bodies: Tracking Immunity in American Culture From the Days of Polio to the Age of AIDS*, is an exceptional example of how research can involve such an integration. She began this work interested in how the body's immune system was constructed within multiple intersecting discourses: the media, the scientific community, traditional and non-traditional medical practitioners, the public imagination, etc. Describing a pivotal moment in her research, Martin noted "one of the clearest moments of 'implosion' in my fieldwork, when elements from different research contexts seemed to collapse into one another with great force, occurred in a graduate course I was taking in immunology . . ." (p. 91). During this moment, she made a connection between the trope of "flexibility" prominent in scientific discourses on the immune system and trope of flexible specialization prominent in theories of late twentieth century capitalism.

This led Martin to design a study that would allow her to understand this connection (and other related connections) more fully. Although not a focus group study per se, Martin's work illustrates nicely the myriad kinds of collective conversations that can emerge when interactions between researchers and research participants are not prefigured but emergent. As such, it represents yet another way to think about focus group work beyond the usual or traditional ways, thus indexing its yet-to-be-discovered potentials.

Martin and her colleagues engaged in many kinds of data collection. To insure that they criss-crossed diverse cultural terrains in a variety of different ways, they entered the social worlds of their participants—"living in [many different kinds of neighborhoods in Baltimore, MD], joining neighborhood associations, attending community meetings, block parties, and festivals, and volunteering to work on neighborhood projects" (p. 9). Many of these social spaces and the activities that occur in them bear strong family resemblances to what we have, throughout this book, called focus groups broadly defined. Additionally, these researchers conducted open-ended conversational interviews with individuals, pairs, and small groups of people. They also conducted all of their research meetings as synergistic focus group activities. Finally, in what we might call postmodern focus group practice, they developed qualitative data analysis software that—at least metaphorically—allowed the content of each conversational interview and focus group to interact with the content of all others. In other words, all transcripts—whether from interviews with individuals, pairs, or small groups—were treated analytically as a

> collectively produced text, a kind of encyclopedia of what a diverse population thinks is sayable, imaginable, or thinkable about health, illness, the body, and society . . . The open-ended nature of the conversations allowed issues and ways of thinking that we could not anticipate to emerge and be heard . . . Both [researcher and research participants] explored issues of mutual concern and interest interpretively . . . The range of community settings in which we worked ensured that they [the participants] would make up a broad cross-section of the society.
>
> (Martin, 1995, p. 10)

Their context sensitive and very inventive research design and data collection and analysis strategies allowed these researchers to see, from different angles, aspects of how health or illness was constructed in many different realms of life and work (e.g. clinics, support groups, research laboratories, medical training programs, corporate settings focusing on healthcare, and alternative medicine practices).

> By becoming involved in all of these settings, [they] sought to put [themselves] in places where [they] would be touched and [they] hoped, propelled by the same processes affecting other people in the society. [They] wanted [their] fieldwork to fetch [them] up in what have been called *implosions*, places where different elements in the system come into energetic contact and collapse in on themselves.
>
> (Martin, 1995, p. 11)

From her many and varied findings, Martin was able to draw connections among the constitutive forces of flexibility in immunology, practices of corporate management, and new ideologies of work in medical-scientific fields, and their embodiment in training programs both in medicine and in basic science educational contexts. Based on these connections, she was able to develop an argument for the emergence of a post-Darwinian public imagination in the United States as a function of these intersecting and co-constituting discourses that on the surface of things seemed "worlds apart." Among other things, this public imagination implied selves or subjectivities that were also post-Darwinian in nature. Participants from across diverse social contexts, cultures, and occupational settings consistently constructed health and illness in terms of a kind of social-cultural-racial survival of the fittest. For example, many people made "comparative estimates about the quality of different people's immune systems" (p. 240) as a function of race or social class. In the end, Martin argued that "what is at stake in our understanding of 'health' are the broadest issues of the survival and death of the social order itself" (p. 240). She went on to show how this argument undergirded various theories of "evolution by training" circulating within cultural studies arenas, Rupert Sheldrake's "morphic resonance" theory (or the hundredth monkey theory), and many very similar folk theories held by many people and purveyed in popular media such as *Time, Newsweek, Esquire,* and *Science Digest.* Finally, Martin demonstrated how these various scientific and folk theories now constitute the foundations for "new capitalist" versions of racism, xenophobia, and social justice.

Disclosing connections in ways like Martin did in this study constitutes a powerful way to suture sites of cultural production that had previously seemed unconnected and thus to create empirically grounded new accounts of intersecting social landscapes and the effects of these intersections. Additionally, Martin's individual and collective conversations, along with her prescient reflections upon these conversations, surfaced synergistic linkages among inquiry, politics, and pedagogy. As we have argued throughout, these linkages are always latent within focus group work, and they often end up disclosing complexities, nuances, and contradictions embodied in "lived experience." They also begin to disclose social and economic forces that often get glossed or explained away by one or another cultural logic. Exploiting these potentials often occurs in focus group work and it is thus particularly effective for making invisible connections between and among constitutive structures and forces visible.

Creating opportunities for solidarity building and political action

In an age when spaces for democratic interactions and the communally enacted social justice agendas are becoming increasingly eclipsed and atomized, focus groups can become transformative democratic spaces for solidarity building and political effectivity. So, another key affordance of focus group work is the promotion of political synergy among participants, which often leads to political activist work. Perhaps the clearest example of focus groups and their role in politically charged work is through participatory action research (PAR) and collaborative action research (CAR). A particularly good example of this kind of research is represented in Eve Tuck's *Urban Youth and School Pushout: Gateways, Get-Aways, and the GED*. According to Tuck, "[r]ather than a set of methods, PAR is best described as an ethic, as a set of beliefs about knowledge, where it comes from, and how knowledge is validated and strengthened" (2012, p. 4). PAR typically involves participants in the entire research process—from the definition of the problem though the research itself through the dissemination of results. Perhaps not surprisingly, focus groups have been used in many PAR projects. Again, Tuck's study is a good example here.

In this study, Tuck examined the GED degree and what it means to the young people who flock to it year after year as an alternative to a traditional high school degree. Among other things, she highlighted the inexhaustible search for "dignity" that pushes many young people out of high schools and into the Byzantine world of this testing apparatus. An especially interesting finding from her work is the fact that young people look to "repatriate" their own educational experiences through the degree. Because her work was unabashedly political, Tuck drew together two contemporary bodies of theory and research with obvious political valences—the postcolonial work of indigenous scholars and the post-structural work of Deleuze and Guattari (e.g. 1987). Each theoretical lens offered a unique angle of vision on the phenomena that interested her most. Using the postcolonial construct of "repatriation" allowed Tuck to see how and why her participants were so bent on carving out some sense of "dignity" in a system designed to rob them of it. Using Deleuze's insights about the fundamental importance of "desire" in all human activity, Tuck was able to see and explain how "desire" was the key motivational mechanism operating in the lives of the youth with whom she worked (i.e. through various kinds of "desiring machines" such as positive face and belonging). The focus group discussions in which she and the young people participated brought to light the fact that desire is neither predictable nor scripted, but essentially free flowing. Importantly, paying attention to the "desiring machines" of these young people allowed schools to take up Tuck's research to change their policies and practices to better meet their needs. Interestingly, this appropriation process also revealed some fault lines that threatened institutional stability in fundamental ways. To their credit, the schools were able to address these threats in productive ways and without jettisoning the positive changes they had made.

Of particular interest to us in this chapter is how Tuck used focus groups in inventive ways. Also drawing on the work of Deleuze and Guattari (1987), Tuck involved her participants in "mapping" projects. Deleuze and Guattari make an important distinction between *tracing* and *mapping*. A tracing is a copy and operates according to "genetic" principles of reproduction based on an a priori deep structure and a faith in the discovery and representation of that structure. Tracings are based on phenomenological experience that is assumed to be essential, stable, and universal. Defined thus, the findings from most research projects are tracings. Deleuze and Guattari use psychoanalysis as an example of a historically powerful regime of truth within which tracings are always at work. No matter what an analysand utters, it is read against Oedipus, the phallus, lack, desire for the mother, rage against the father, etc. In contrast to tracings, maps are open systems—contingent, unpredictable, and productive.

> The map is open and connectable in all of its dimensions; it is detachable, reversible, susceptible to constant modification. It can be torn, reversed, adapted, to any kind of mounting, reworked by an individual, group, or social formation to fit their purposes . . . A map has multiple entryways, as opposed to the tracing, which always comes back to the same.
>
> (Deleuze and Guattari, 1987, pp. 12–15)

They go on to suggest that the creation of maps (as opposed to tracings) provides more sophisticated understandings of the development, maintenance, and rearticulation of social institutions. In drawing maps, the theorist works at the surface, "creating" possible realities by producing new articulations of disparate phenomena and connecting the exteriority of objects to whatever forces or directions seem potentially related to them. As such, maps exceed both individual and collective experiences of what seems "naturally" real. Deleuze and Guattari suggest that after constructing maps, one may then place more apparently stable tracings back onto them, interrogating breaks and fissures where one finds them. Ultimately, a map produces an organization of reality rather than reproducing some prior description or theorization of it.

In one mapping activity, Tuck worked with her participants to create "problem tree" maps. This activity was designed to explore and document the ways young people understood complex phenomena in their lives like the GED. They represented their emerging knowledge in terms of roots and branches. Their "problem trees" were ways for young people to think through three levels of analysis in looking at a problem—the leaves or the "everyday symptoms of the problem," the trunk or the "common beliefs and assumptions that support the leaves," and the roots or the "ideologies that structure the whole tree" (Tuck, 2008, p. 49). One remarkable outcome of their mapping work was the devaluation of the GED—a devaluation grounded in connections they drew among the money allotted to prisons over and above schools, the popular media that stresses hierarchies between people, and the privatization of public space (2008, p. 111). Tuck also engaged the youth in several other kinds of mapping activities in the context of focus groups, including mapping the structures and forces responsible for the apparent naturalness of school push out and meritocracy (2012, p. 6). Importantly, these connections and the map that produced them were collectively generated in focus groups, and Tuck attributed much of the success of her work to the intellectual and political synergy they afford, even demand. Tuck's PAR work, then, is a telling example of how PAR and CAR—which pivot on political synergy becoming political activism—often depend upon focus group activity for their success.

Conclusions

In this chapter we have focused on the key affordances of focus group work. These include: mitigating the researcher's authority and generating deeper understandings; disclosing the constitutive power of discourse and the lifeblood of social activity; approximating the natural; filling in knowledge gaps and saturating understanding; drawing out complexity, nuance, and contradiction; disclosing eclipsed or invisible connections; and creating opportunities for solidarity building and political action. Taken together, these affordances highlight many of the reasons why the specificities and autonomies of focus group work allow researchers to excavate information from participants that they would never be able to excavate using other data collection strategies.

We would like to offer some forward-looking thoughts on these affordances and the relation between and among them. First, as we think is obvious when reading through this chapter, the affordances we discussed can and do overlap with each other. For example, mitigating the researcher's authority often helps to generate deeper understandings that can and do draw out complexity, nuance, and contradiction. We have only separated out the affordances heuristically so that we could present them in a coherent, readily digestible way. In actual practice, how affordances interact with each other is much less tidy and much more complex—intersecting, overlapping, and mutually reinforcing each other in myriad ways. Second, these affordances underscore the expansive and ecumenical definition of focus groups that we have tried to develop throughout this book. While most discussions of focus groups have, in effect, defined them a priori, we have done something different. We have emphasized neither the form of focus groups nor the procedures for conducting them. Instead, we have emphasized their potentials—what they afford in terms of unearthing rich data sets that most other data collection strategies do not afford (or afford as well). Among other things, this shift in emphasis has allowed us to think through studies that have not been marked specifically as "focus group" research as traditionally defined. For example, we think *Slim's Table* is a good example of a study conducted from within the Chicago School trajectory and the methods used by Chicago School scholars. Recall that these scholars were particularly interested in how communities are developed and maintained through habituated patterns of talk and social interaction. But the various forms of collective discourse that constitute the data for *Slim's Table* also provides insights into some of the best impulses of focus group work, as well as the kinds of myriad collective conversations we might call focus groups. A more expansive approach to conceptualizing focus groups and focus group research allows us *both* to read studies like *Slim's Table* anew *and* to think about the nature and functions of focus groups anew. Focusing on affordances rather than on form or procedure has also allowed us to see the many forms of social interaction that can emerge from focus group conversations, as well as the myriad effects of these forms. Third, emphasizing affordances has allowed us to highlight the inherent multifunctionality of focus groups—the ways they allow for outcomes that are simultaneously pedagogical, political, and research-oriented, as well as how lines between and among these three functions are blurred at best in actual practice. For example, mitigating the authority of the focus group facilitator or drawing out nuance, complexity, and contradiction are all very much a part of research, pedagogy, and political activism. Finally, using the word "affordance" itself is a matter of hedging our claims. None of these "affordances" are "inherent" to a particular research strategy or approach. Conceivably, for example, some of these affordances could play out using one-on-one interviews or even surveys. Still, based on our review of the literature and our own research experience, we are confident that the affordances we have discussed emerge much more often and in more powerful ways in focus groups compared to most (perhaps all) other modes of data collection. Why focus groups draw out these affordances in unique and uniquely powerful ways seems related to how performative they are and how the performances they spawn recapitulate naturally occurring social activity.

In Chapter 4 we turn to a more practical discussion of how we have used focus groups in our own research. The goal of this chapter is to offer models for how focus groups might be used by others. Because we offer recommendations for exploiting the affordances of focus groups in this chapter, its tone is a bit more didactic than the tone of the first three chapters of this book. We do not, however, mean to be prescriptive here. Our suggestions should be taken heuristically, as food for thought in designing and conducting new research projects that are both rigorous and inventive and that perhaps lead to the discovery of elements of effective focus group work that the qualitative research community has not yet encountered or imagined.

Chapter 4

Fundamental elements of effective focus group research practice

As we have noted, focus group research almost always involves contingent, synergistic articulations of three functions: inquiry, politics, and pedagogy. Recall that we have used the imaginal metaphor of the prism to think about these functions and relations. Our work with focus groups has indeed been prismatic, and several key principles or highly recommended practices for facilitating rigorous, synergistic, effective research using focus groups have emerged from this prismatic work. In this chapter, we unpack these principles, and we demonstrate how they have played out in our own research. These include: exploiting pre-existing social networks that encourage collegiality; doing our best to create safe, comfortable, and even festive spaces "of" the people; using open-ended prompts for questions and then letting group participants "take over"; keeping notes and following up on key themes and gaps; listening for breakdowns and subtexts and asking for elaboration. Finally, expect unpredictable group dynamics and even conflict and contradiction. These can be particularly productive affordances of focus group work.

We unpack these principles and their effects by discussing key moments or activities from studies we have conducted, most notably (a) a study of urban youth responding to African American media culture (specifically hip hop) and (b) a study of how immigrant women from Mexico responded to the exigencies of their new life in the Midwestern United States. Because these projects were distinct in several ways, discussing them in tandem allows us to construct a subtext that further helps build our argument about the need to think about and practice focus groups in increasingly expansive, ecumenical ways. Perhaps most obviously, the intentionality involved in defining and implementing focus groups. In the latter project, George drew together female adult immigrants to have discussions about the conditions of their lives in their new Midwest home. Focus groups, here, were chosen as a distinct information gathering tools because of their particular affordances. Partially because of the intentionality involved here, the focus group conversations from this study yielded rich, extended transcripts—large chunks of recorded talk where the most relevant contextual information can be read off the talk itself. The former study (conducted by Greg with George as doctoral advisor and research partner for a portion of the time) was conducted over a four-year period at a community center, with follow-up work with key participants lasting two years beyond that point (see Dimitriadis, 2001, for a fuller discussion of this project). The participants were adolescents and teenagers. The focus groups, here, were always embedded within other social activities (such as listening to music or viewing films). Therefore, the transcripts yielded from these focus groups are much more fragmentary, fractured and incomplete, requiring much more contextual information to understand fully. Additionally, because of how the project was structured, focus group activity often occurred in tandem with natural, everyday interactions and activities between and among participants, as well as other modes of data collection—observations, queries to individuals, and artifact generation and collection. The constant overlapping of everyday activity and research activity and the simultaneous use of a variety of data collection lenses and strategies allowed Greg to develop a deeply ethnographic perspective on the data and eventually to construct a rich ethnographic account of what he learned about his participants and their world(s). Such perspectives and accounts could not be constructed in George's study of new immigrant women largely because data were collected almost entirely in focus groups (although some observations were conducted at relevant sites and individual interviews were conducted with some women and service providers in the community). Taken together, our discussions of these two very differently designed studies in the service of illustrating the key principles of effective focus group work provide some sense of the extent and range ways one might deploy focus groups in research. Additionally, because the same key principles for effective focus group work emerged from these two very differently designed studies, the validity of these principles and their functions is enhanced.

Building upon and extending pre-existing social networks

Exploiting pre-existing social networks also contributes to the success of focus group work. Recall in this regard our discussion of Janice Radway's (1984) groundbreaking ethnographic research on women's investments in romance novels. Assisted by the bookstore owner (Dot), Radway played into the ongoing activity dynamics of existing networks of women who were avid readers of romance novels. She simply "formalized" some of their ongoing activities with her focus groups. In doing so, she was able to generate more systematic and rich accounts about the social circumstances that motivated the women's investments in romance novels, the nature and purposes of their specific reading practices, their attitudes toward issues and themes salient in the novels, their reading styles and preferences, and multiple and contradictory functions of romance reading among the women she studied.

In their first efforts to get their focus group study of immigrant women off the ground, George and his colleagues distributed flyers through various Latino venues such as churches, Mexican grocery stores, the Latino Coalition building, and the local YWCA where they planned to hold the focus groups. Very few women showed up for the first few focus groups, and little synergy developed among those who did. Reflecting upon this failure, George decided to ask a few participants with whom he and his colleagues had begun to develop good relationships what social activities they engaged in (e.g. church, discussion groups, work) and whether they would invite some of their friends and colleagues from those activity settings to participate in our focus groups. As it turned out, participants who joined the groups via such invitations were much more excited about the focus group conversations; they were the ones who attended most frequently; they were the ones who shared their personal experiences most fully; and they were the ones who eventually assumed leadership roles both in the focus groups and in social activist efforts spawned by the focus groups.

Greg conducted a study of adolescents' investments in popular culture, which he came to call RAPPS for Real Art, Politics and Poetry Sessions. This study unfolded a bit differently from George's with respect to the existing social networks. Interested in young people's responses to hip hop, he gathered participants for his study from a local community center in the Midwest. In contrast to George's study where recruiting participants was the first step, Greg's study began with the choice of a site. This meant embedding the focus groups as part of the ongoing programming at the site. In fact, integrating focus group discussions with other activities happening at the center was a key part of gaining access to the site. Once access was granted, the content of the program was negotiated with the unit director of the site, Johnny. Johnny was explicit from the outset that the program should serve multiple purposes—give young people a chance to talk about hip hop, serve as part of the site's educational programming, and provide food for the youth involved (more on this later). After becoming familiar with many of the goals, activities, personnel, and young people at the site, Greg was able to draw on pre-existing friendship networks—small groups of young people who tended to hang out together and engage in the same activities (including the RAPPS sessions) at the same times. Because these groups were already formed and relatively stable, Greg did not need to engage in aggressive or creative recruitment efforts. The key was getting the popular and longstanding unit director, Johnny, on board. This needed to be done with some sensitivity. In fact, this project began as a class project for George's two-semester qualitative research class. When Greg and George discussed what he might do for the class, George pulled out a phone book to look for addresses of community centers. He also suggested going in personally and not sending a letter in advance. This was good advice. It contributed to developing a personal relationship with Johnny, which turned out to be very important because such relationships were part of the ethos of the center. Playing into this ethos, albeit unwittingly, was a crucial first step in developing a process of negotiation that pivoted on reciprocity. Indeed this process of negotiation unfolded in very similar ways in relation to a variety of different activities and projects conducted at the center during the next several years.

Even though exploiting pre-existing social networks has a history of effective-ness in the literature on focus group research, and even though we have had considerable success using pre-existing social networks in our own research, sampling in all kinds of research (including focus group research) should always be done purposively and strategically. We can certainly imagine studies in which it would make perfect sense to include participants who represent the entire political or social spectrum of an issue under study. Similarly, in other studies one might choose to include participants who seem diametrically opposed to each other with respect to the topic under study or who are positioned (socially, economically, politically, etc.) in very different ways with respect to the focus of the research.

As with many aspects of focus group research (as well as research more broadly), it is a question of modulating decisions and effects. For example, Greg's study initially attracted certain friendship networks of which key gang members in the community were a part. This was certainly helpful in getting the groups up and running. But it is worth considering whether these members had disproportional effects on group discussions with concomitant consequences for the kinds of information gathered. What might have happened if Greg and George had more self-consciously organized these groups or recruited young people from outside of the center to join them? What kinds of discussions might have unfolded if white youth interested in rap and hip hop were in the groups? At the very least, we would imagine quite different kinds of discussions—perhaps ones that embodied a richer, more diverse set of perspectives. But maybe not. Maybe class and race differences or the fact that social networks were disrupted or any number of other factors would have suppressed participants' willingness to share their thoughts and feelings. Whatever outcome might have emerged from these imagined scenarios, our main point here is that focus groups allow for explicit modulations of participants and participation in ways that many (probably most) other methods do not.

Creating safe spaces for interaction and self-disclosure

It is extremely important to create safe and comfortable spaces *for* and *of* the participants. When George and his colleagues began the study of immigrant women, they arranged a meeting in the YWCA building where some of the women took English as a Second Language (ESL) classes. Although quite a few women showed up and none complained about the space, they did not seem comfortable. After a couple of sessions and considerable attrition, the Spanish-speaking facilitator asked the remaining participants why they thought others had apparently dropped out. They told her that they were not satisfied with the ESL classes they had paid for and that the building where they took these classes was not a place they enjoyed being in. The facilitator asked them where they would like to meet. Participants suggested meeting in each other's homes on a rotating basis. From that day on, focus groups were held in participants' homes and some-times in community sites where they got together (e.g. churches, community centers) and felt comfortable. Not only did gathering in these kinds of spaces (as well as doing other things to create community and solidarity which we discuss later on in the chapter) encourage some of our apparent dropouts to return, it also facilitated participants' senses of feeling *at home* in the discussions; it helped to build trust between and among other participants and the researchers; and it eventually led even the most reticent participants to open up and to disclose information that was both relevant and very personal. In relation to this last point, one of the focus group sessions about two months into the study was held in the home of a woman who was a very good friend of this most reticent participant. During this session, this participant "confessed" having a learning disability and talked about the long-term negative effects it had on her confidence and self-esteem. This "confession" led other women in the group to share stories that they had previously glossed over or not shared at all. Although not the only reason for this breakthrough, the fact that the session in which it occurred was held in a best friend's house seemed to contribute to a certain degree of safety and comfort that allowed this usually reticent participant to open up and share painful personal experiences.

In a conversation that was going on as we were settling in for another focus group session, Elana and Carmen were discussing "the lack of continuity" in the ESL classes they were taking and suggesting that the program should have different groups for students at different proficiency levels and quasi-mandatory attendance so that teachers had the same students each week. The facilitator of the session asked them to share what they had been discussing with the whole group. This invitation led to a long discussion of "*acceptation en la comunidad*," of which a segment is reproduced here:

ELANA: I don't like LARA English classes because they don't have continuity.

CARMEN: The teachers have new students every class.

LOLITA: And they have volunteers, not real teachers.

ANTONIA: They should make different groups for different levels [of English].

ROSARIO: University Church has an ESL program.

CARMEN: But it's very expensive, about $70.

LOLITA: I went for one level, the first level, and I liked it. It was very funny. But they don't have childcare, and you have to pay parking.

CARMEN: Faith Baptist Church has classes for $20, and a really good teacher.

ELANA: I want to learn English, and LARA is easy for me to get to.

ANTONIA: Me too. People laugh at me when I speak English. When my husband is talking to an American, I understand a lot, but when the American talks to me, I get confused and don't understand one word.

ELANA: I only finished elementary school in Mexico because I had learning problems in Spanish. I can only learn English if I have a very good teacher. In Mexico they teach pronouns in secondary school. If I never learned what a pronoun is in Spanish, how can I learn it in English without a good teacher? But I want to learn English because I could earn more money and live better. Some people say we should learn English because we are in America. But what those people forget is that learning a second language takes time. The problem is, in the mean time, before we learn, they should help us.

CLARITA: And the Americans in banks and doctors' offices should learn some Spanish or have translators.

CARMEN: We should ask the Latino Coalition people to say this.

This conversation continued for some time with several other women sharing snippets of their educational experiences in Mexico, "confessing" low levels of success in school, and expressing worries about their own children's acceptance in American schools and the quality of instruction in English they were getting. In short, these women shared very important "secrets," and their sharing motivated the beginnings of some very important activist work. We will return to these issues in other sections of the chapter. Our main point here has been to emphasize how critically important it is to create safe and comfortable spaces for focus group activity and to suggest that these spaces are not epiphenomenal but constitutive of highly successful focus group work.

The issue of "space" was also central to Greg's study. Most specifically, holding conversations with youth at a local community center that was almost a "second home" for them allowed for conversations that quite likely would not have happened in other settings such as public schools, which were spaces where many young people had not had many positive experiences. Community centers designed for children and youth tend to draw on the pre-existing strengths of young people rather than judging them against some arbitrary (and typically socially conservative) yardstick for development, which usually renders many of them "deficient" in relation to the yardstick. This was certainly the case in the RAPPS work. Young people who had been marginalized at school saw the community center as a "safe space." In particular, the center had a long history in the local community, and many of the staff members were community fixtures and icons. Holding RAPPS sessions at the center thus allowed for discussions that were educational but not marked by the alienating dimensions of "schooling." This became important for the set of discussions about film and history Greg and George had with the young people in their sessions.

More specifically, they conducted a series of discussions of contemporary films related to African American history. Although they eventually focused on the film *Panther* (about the Black Panther Party for Self Defense), they briefly discussed *X* (about Malcolm X), and *Rosewood* (about an all-black town targeted by white supremacists in the early twentieth century). These discussions were quite different from similar discussions about similar topics that these same young people experienced in school where teachers tended to sanction and censor topics, focusing, for example, only on key icons such as Martin Luther King and addressing only his non-violence orientation. Key issues in their lives—such as poor relationships with the police or racial profiling in local establishments—were never broached. In connection with this point, the community center served an almost wholly African American population and was a valued and valuable resource in the community. As such, it existed in sharp distinction to the local public schools that the young people had to attend.

As it turned out, providing opportunities for young people to connect cultural history—like that represented in *Panther*—to their own experiences in ways not allowed or encouraged in school was extremely important. Among other things, these opportunities gave participants a different angle of vision on learning and thus a different angle of vision on how education might figure into their possible futures.

In sum, space matters. In both of the studies we discussed, where we held our focus groups had consequences both for attracting participants and for the kinds and amounts of information we were able to gather. The women in George's study expressed a strong preference for meeting in their homes. They felt safe and comfortable in these spaces, and once we began meeting in them, our groups got larger and more stable, sensitive topics emerged in conversations more often, and personal emotional floodgates began to open. In the study of African American urban youth, the fact that participants were already socially and emotionally connected to the community center where we held our focus groups and the fact that they trusted its adult leaders were crucial. These factors helped get discussions of history, race, racism, culture, and violence off the ground. Although we do not know for sure, we have pretty good evidence to suggest that the kinds of rich, heartfelt, complex discussions that unfolded at the center would not have unfolded in even close to similar ways had we held our sessions at a local public school. In this regard, it is telling that our participants were so willing to engage in pedagogical activities at the center even when they told us they resisted the very same kinds of activities in school.

Expecting (even celebrating) contingency, unpredictability, and contradiction

Although this may seem counterintuitive, one should expect (even celebrate) contingent group dynamics, conflict, and even contradiction during focus group sessions, especially early on in any study. Although these dimensions of social interaction are a bit scary and difficult to manage, they often surface issues that would remain buried if tensions and attempts to address them were not allowed to occur. In George's study with new immigrant women in the United States, several highly contested discussions occurred around work and marriage that led to rich, productive discussions and even political activist work in relation to gender roles and relations, and working conditions at manufacturing plants. In what follows, we present transcript snippets from focus group interactions and then discuss their import.

In a discussion about problems with mobility and transportation it quickly became apparent that this seemingly straightforward issue was anything but straightforward. The following transcript begins to bring this social fact into view:

ELANA: Public transportation is a big problem here. The buses don't come often. You need to wait one hour if you miss one. And there is no bus at 6am when I go to work.

FACILITATOR: So, how do you get to work?

ELANA: I usually get a ride from someone else that has a car.

CARMEN: Who gives you a ride?

ELANA: I get a ride from J or B. It costs a lot, $30 a week. And you never know if they will come or not until the time they are supposed to pick you up, and if they don't show up, you probably will lose the day, and then you lose the payment for this day.

ANTONIA: I think the Mexicans who have been in this country a long time take advantage of the ones that have only been here a little while. Some charge $400 to fill out a job application.

CARMEN: I don't work far from Wabash. I could give you a ride.

CLARITA: I have a car too.

ELANA: And I would like to learn how to drive.

MARGARITA: I would like to drive too, but my husband won't let me get a license. He doesn't think it is important. He doesn't let me do lots of things. I would like to work too.

When George and his colleagues asked about transportation issues faced by the women in this study, what they thought would unfold was a discussion about practical difficulties in getting to work, getting children to doctors, and so on. What actually ended up happening was an unearthing of many *invisible* dimensions of the lived experiences of these women that were far more critical than the practical problems they faced. For example, it became clear that there was quite a bit of exploitation within this community of immigrants—a community consisting primarily of people from the same region (even town) in Mexico and one that, on the surface, seemed quite cohesive and collectively determined to contribute to the viability of their emerging ethnic enclave in a fairly hostile social environment. It also became clear that these women faced some serious gender-related problems in their lives. Not only were most businesses run by men who exploited their customers (including our participants), but their husbands, too, were oppressing them. Additionally, besides affecting their senses of self-worth, being controlled by their husbands, not having licenses, and not having ready access to other forms of transportation also affected their ability to participate as fully as they would have liked in their children's school activities, to work outside the home, and even to fulfill their gender-related domestic responsibilities efficiently. Surfacing these issues and their causes, as well as how the focus groups became stepping stones for activist work in relation to them, came as a surprise to us. So did the effects of their activist work, which we discuss later on in the chapter in relation to some other key principles of effective focus group work.

As we mentioned earlier in this chapter, Greg developed various "prompts" (e.g. provocative quotations from hip hop icons, photographs, songs, magazine articles) to initiate discussions during the RAPPS sessions. As we also mentioned, he suggested that the groups view and discuss several films focused on African American history—*X*, *Rosewood*, and *Panther*. In response to this suggestion the contingent, unpredictable nature of focus group work became highly visible. As became clear right from the start and continued despite our various efforts to generate interest in them, *X* and *Rosewood* were not films these young people had any interest in watching and talking about. They were seen as too "school like." They were unappealing because they embodied very little action and because they were "boring" stories about individual icons (as in *X*) or more drawn-out historical events (as in *Rosewood*). In contrast, *Panther* featured an action-driven plot that revolved around a "gang-like" group—the Black Panthers. In addition, the film featured lots of scenes of the Panthers fighting back against the police. As we mentioned earlier, the community in which these young people lived did not have entirely positive relations with the police. This film gave voice to those tensions, allowing participants to engage with it in deeply personal and cultural ways. *Panther* also had a very empowering message for these youth, even as they struggled to understand legacy of the Panthers. One older member in one of the sessions expressed this struggle nicely as he communicated his understanding of the Panthers—one that connected the Panthers to Malcolm X, Martin Luther King, and even gangs:

> In a way it's a lot different from gangs, but they was about trying to get equal rights. To me it was like Martin Luther King and Malcolm X, the two combined. They was like Malcolm X because when the police starts beating them, they believe in hitting back. And like Martin Luther King, because they believe in equal rights for everybody. Martin Luther King because they believe in equal right for all blacks and then. Malcolm X because they believe if the police was hitting you, you had the right to hit them back. That's why they had the guns, the constitutional right to bear arms.

When Greg asked him to elaborate on the connection between the Panthers and gangs, a topic that had already come up many times in earlier discussions, this participant noted:

> I kind of see where they coming from, 'cause they see the guns, and they see . . . Even though they ain't buying the guns, but they see the guns, and they see most gang members with guns, but they see the guns, and they see most gang members with guns, so therefore it put them in the mind of gangs. And then they got a little click like the gangs got.

Both examples shared in this section highlighted moments or events when contingency, unpredictability, and contradiction became our allies in the research process. Although we advise having a well-developed research plan for any study using focus groups (or any study period), we also advise paying attention to "surprises." Because of the dynamic, performative nature of much focus group activity, many unexpected things are likely to happen in them. Finding ways to explore and exploit the contingent, the unpredictable, and the contradictory almost always discloses important new dimensions of participants' knowledge and experience and thus results in fuller and richer data sets.

Using open-ended prompts and allowing participants to direct conversations

Using prompts (not questions) that are maximally open-ended and that allow participants to *take over* discussions almost always result in richer and more complex conversations that often result in significant learning and political activity. For example, in George's study of the challenges faced by immigrant women in the United States, the focus group conversation about mobility and transportation issues that we discussed in the previous section began quite slowly, revolved primarily around the scarcity of public transportation in their small rural community, and after about half an hour seemed to be dissolving into little more than a "gripe" session. A bit frustrated, the session facilitator asked participants a very simple, open-ended question: "What do you suppose you could do to make it easier for you to get the transportation services you need?" Instead of answering our question, they began to disclose a whole host of oppressive forces in their lives. They talked about underground car services run by entrepreneurial Mexican American men that were both unreliable and very expensive. In discussing these problems, participants surfaced even more serious problems such as sexism and economic exploitation within the Mexican American community. They went on to talk about the fracturing effects these forces had on community solidarity. Within weeks of the initial discussion of this transportation problem, a group of women created a co-op ride sharing system. This system grew and became more efficient over time. Among other things, the co-op forced mercenary drivers to lower their fees.

The women also instigated discussions of sexism that emerged in the initial focus group sessions, especially the oppression resulting because many husbands discouraged (even prevented) their wives from getting licenses. In about a year, women who had licenses began to teach women who did not have licenses how to drive and arranged for them to take their driving tests. Now, although we celebrate these efforts, it should be obvious to all readers that they also embody the potential to usher in serious problems with respect to dominant and marginalized people within relationships, organizations, and communities.

The Panther study also revealed something important about the relation between prompts and the interactional dynamics of focus groups. At several points, Greg asked the youth what part of the film they liked best. To a person, all of the youth said that they liked the ways the Panthers fought back against the police. Comments such as "I like when he called them Pig" and "I was surprised the police were scared" were common. As we have suggested throughout, this anti-police subtext was an important one because it indexed participants abiding fears and concerns. Talk about their abiding fears and concerns most often surfaced in response to very open-ended questions.

Additionally, open-ended questions also helped us develop follow-up questions that allowed the youth to expand upon their ideas about the relations between the texts we were discussing and their own lives. For example, although the youth talked about the police in relation to *Panther* quite a bit, it took some time and coming at the issue from several different angles to get them to unpack the many ways that they linked their emerging knowledge of the Black Panthers ways of dealing with the police (including having more knowledge of the constitution than the police and using that knowledge strategically) and the police presence in their own neighborhoods.

Asking maximally open-ended questions and stepping back so that our participants could run with them also allowed us to see other aspects of context that contributed to the evocation of rich conversations. For example, *Panther* as text contributed to structuring the young people's focus and the modulation of their talk. For example, there was a subtext in the film that had to do with the FBI allowing drugs to be imported into Oakland to quell incipient political activity. None of the segments embodying this subtext came up in discussions generated through asking open-ended questions. When we attempted to ask about this subtext more directly, students had no interest in talking about them, and our discussions fell flat. Because these subtextual aspects of the film interested us, we paid closer attention to how our participants interacted with the film. We noticed that they seemed to tune out and often began taking to each other about unrelated issues during such segments—the so-called "talking parts." Had our questions been less open-ended and had we not allowed our participants to engage in viewing and discussing the film in *their* ways rather than our *ways*, we do not think we would have realized how various dimensions of context (such as the filmic structure of *Panther*) contributed to these young people's reception practices. Nor would we have learned as much as we did about what they found compelling (and not compelling) about the various texts (magazine articles, songs, photographs, films) we read/viewed/listened to and discussed together.

Even more interestingly, the discussions that seemed most focused and productive to us while we were facilitating the sessions often seemed the least interesting and productive in retrospect. In contrast, the discussions that were more free-flowing and rhizomatic—ones that we thought in the moment were out-of-control, off task, and tangential to our interests—often yielded the most penetrating insights about how our participants understood *Panther* (and other media texts) and how they related these texts to other cultural resources and to their own lives. For example and as we will discuss in more detail later on in the chapter, there was a clear and coherent logic to our participants' surprising and unpredictable conversations about gangs, other films featuring large African American casts, and professional wrestling. Understanding this logic was a struggle for us. In the moment, we thought they were just jumping from one topic to another and avoiding the issues we were asking them to talk about. We were frustrated because their conversations seemed unfocused and unproductive. We were tempted to be more heavy-handed and directive in facilitating the conversations. We are glad we did not though because these kinds of conversations turned out to be anything but unfocused and unproductive. We simply could not see the sophisticated connections our participants were making—connections that only became clear to us much later and after much analysis and reflection. The lesson in all of this is that although relinquishing control of the flow of talk and social interaction during focus groups often feels risky and uncomfortable, it often results in intense and productive conversations that produce abundant, rich, complexly textured, counterintuitive data and insights.

Cultivating *communitas*

Also crucial in focus group work is to create a sense of the communal and to celebrate collective togetherness. In this regard, focus group activity is not unlike the kind of community process of renewal analyzed by Victor Turner (1969). In his analysis, the process is rooted in a crucial "betwixt and between" state that tends to summon up fundamental first principles by abrogating everyday life patterns. As such, this activity has the power to reactivate the sense of *communitas* that authorizes the quotidian of communal structure. The interpersonal, communal behavior of all participants, in which the very elements of mutual human faith, understanding, and cooperation are precariously at stake yet always affirmed is this archetypal analogue of marginality (solidarity in oppression). Such analogues often serve as points of departure and ways of proceeding that disclose the real and significant coherence of any number of apparent anomalies.

Turner's particular conception of liminality is instructive here as well. He conceptualizes liminality as a fertile, ambiguous kind of *neither/both*, which he describes as an elusive fullness of experience that is neither *either/or* (as in either good or evil, either cunning or stupid) nor *both/and* (a category that implies the possibility of resolution and hence reduces the tension that is both elusive and full). Instead, it is a margin which is both worlds it participates in but really, completely neither of them.

Focus groups can and often do create *communitas* and this experience of *neither/both* for their participants. But for this to happen requires both an openness to these possibilities and some planning. But isn't planning for building *communitas* and the experience of neither-both paradoxical, even oxymoronic? Not necessarily. Initiating simple things like down time for casual conversation and getting to know each other and sharing meals together can be very effective for getting these processes/practices in motion. George's work with new immigrant women is particularly instructive here. In this study, he and his colleagues never rushed focus groups or launched right into focused questioning. Instead, they allowed participants to have plenty of time for socializing; they encouraged participants to introduce themselves to each other in non-formal ways; they took long breaks with coffee, tea and snacks during which time participants always mingled and engaged in animated conversations; these conversations ranged in topic from sharing announcements of birthdays, anniversaries, and the like to advertising community events, free services (e.g. mammogram or cholesterol screenings), or job opportunities to talking about cars that are for sale or apartments for rent; finally, they always ended early so that participants could interact with each other in whatever ways they choose, including pursuing topics initiated during breaks. We cannot underscore the importance of these occasions for socializing and social networking for the success of ongoing focus groups. Often these interactions lead to building relationships and planning shared activities in the community. And, for research purposes, they set the scene for gathering rich, pertinent information about our research foci.

As in families, shared meals constitute powerful social glue. The focus groups in the study of new immigrant women (and most studies that both of us have ever conducted) always involved sharing meals. Early on in the study, George and his colleagues made sure to have snacks available during focus group meetings. Although his participants seemed grateful and ate what was provided, they did no seem especially enthusiastic. So the group facilitators asked the women if they would like different kinds of food. Their response was unexpected and surprising. They said that *they* wanted to bring the food. From then on, each session included potluck dinners, where each participant could bring something to share with others. Both spontaneously and in follow-up interviews the women could not say enough about the joy they felt in bringing one of their specialties or a dish based on a new recipe they had tried. Sharing favorite homemade dishes led to relationships (among participants and between participants and researchers) that were increasingly trusting, close, and reciprocally rewarding. This had important implications for how focus group conversations unfolded over time and what kinds and amounts of data were generated from them. We discuss some of these implications/effects in several of the remaining sections of this chapter.

Food was a very important element in Greg's study at the community center as well. In fact, it turned out that "bringing food for the kids" was a prerequisite for access to the club as a site for research. The issue of providing food for participants—pizza at first—was raised at the very first meeting Greg had with Johnny and other senior staff at the center, during which time they made it very clear that part of our responsibility in an emerging collaboration would be to feed our participants and (as we soon learned) center staff as well. In traditional anthropological terms, it became central to patterns of "gift exchange" that developed between Greg, the participants, Johnny, and the club itself. The senior staff member who had initially raised the issue of providing food also encouraged (read: instructed) Greg to bring more pizza than was strictly necessary. Key here is the social fact that everybody involved at the center believed that everybody should "get something" from everybody else based mostly on unsaid or implied assumptions. Food was very much a part of this general ethos, and it was very much linked to building trust between outsiders like Greg and George, the participants, and the staff. That *food* was a key commodity in the "gift exchange" process underscored the fact that reciprocity should respond to and fulfill real needs. This club served a mostly poor, African American population. That Greg brought food every week was not only symbolic, it also filled a real need and thus went a long way in building authentic relations of trust, respect, and reciprocity.

We conclude this section with some thoughts about how the differences in how *communitas* was enacted in the two studies discussed highlights how reciprocity cannot always be predicted in advance. Authentic reciprocity is just that—shared and authentic. It must be negotiated. How each negotiation process unfolds is almost always unique to specific sites and participants, especially with respect to their values and the exigencies of their lives. In the study of new immigrant women, reciprocity began from noticing and responding to a subtext of group dynamics. It grew and flourished because ownership of its lineaments was shared. In the study of urban youth's investments in popular culture, reciprocity began when Greg immediately keyed in on part of the *ethos* of the community center. It grew and flourished as he came to understand this *ethos* more fully and as he developed relationships of respect and trust with center staff and clients.

Paying attention and following up

Keeping careful notes on key themes and concerns that emerge during focus group sessions but are not fully addressed and putting these themes and concerns back on the table in subsequent sessions often excavates important but sensitive topics that participants might shy away from or gloss if they are not reminded about them and asked to elaborate on them. In George's study of immigrant women, the facilitators noticed that the women often talked about medical issues, doctors, clinics, and the like during break times and before and after focus group sessions. They tried a few times to put these topics on the table in a direct way but with little success. The women did not want to talk about them with us. One day, however, the women were talking about pregnancies, children, and related topics in the moments before we were to begin the "official" focus group conversation. Because they seemed happy and spirited, the facilitator imagined they might be more willing than usual to discuss their issues with doctors and healthcare in the community. Rather than approach these subjects directly, she expressed an interest in the conversation they were having about pregnancies, children, and the like. One of the women in the group shared a story about one of her pregnancies, especially the difficulties she had getting the kind of care she wanted and thought she deserved. Soon, the room was buzzing with stories:

LORENA: Going to the doctor costs too much. When I was pregnant, I didn't go to all the visits because of the costs.

ROSARIO: Many pregnant women don't go to the doctor because they cannot afford it.

CARMEN: And when I do go, I cannot explain what I need, and no one is there to translate. They want you to bring your own translator. There are even ads for this in the reception areas.

ANTONIA: Some people have their children translate for them.

MARGARITA: And the doctors get very frustrated when you don't know English well.

CARMEN: They have really bad attitudes toward people that don't speak English very well.

CLARITA: I know someone that has cancer, but it took many months to diagnose her due to language barriers. And when my mother was in the hospital, I went to visit her and she was crying because she didn't eat. She couldn't eat what the nurse gave her, but she didn't know how to say this in English. Nobody tried to find a translator for her or to call a family member.

ELANA: But I don't like to share health problems with my friends. And I don't want to have to depend on a coworker to translate when I go to the doctor . . . because the next day at my work, all the people would be talking about my problem . . . that I got some infection because my husband was with another woman or whatever.

MARGARITA: I don't even tell the doctors all my problems because I am embarrassed.

CLARITA: What about confidentiality?

ANTONIA: They don't care about confidentiality.

ELANA: At the Community Health Clinic they will not take care of more than three medical problems per visit. The doctor told my mother he could not attend all her problems one time—her back and her finger. Then I decided to focus on my mother back problems. She had a car accident when she was entering the US, and she was in pain.

CLARITA: A lot of Mexicans don't know their rights or they are afraid of making more questions if they do not understand the situation or the language very well. I think this is a cultural thing. I have met many Mexicans that have had a job accident and that are very grateful with their supervisors because they drove them to the hospital, they explained things, and they paid medical expenses. But, they did not give them sick days. Those workers were working the day after the accident. We need to teach them to fight for their rights. We are talking about human rights.

Because the research team sensed that getting proper medical care for themselves and their families was highly problematic, facilitators tried many time to surface meaningful talk about this issue. As noted, they had a hard time getting participants to take up these invitations for many months. In research team discussions, they often strategized ways to be more effective in getting the women to talk about the issue. Many of their strategic efforts failed as well. They did not, however, forget their desire to learn more about participants' struggles with the healthcare system. They continued to look for openings to explore the topic. The transcript we just shared represents the first real breakthrough they had in this regard. As the study continued, floodgates opened with respect to this issue. There were many more rich discussions of participants' experiences with healthcare. Even more importantly, the women in the groups began to take action on what they believed to be their basic "human rights." We discuss some of this activist work in another section on of this chapter. Additionally, because "paying attention and following up" was so inextricably connected to noticing and responding to *subtexts* and *breakdowns*, we also return to the issue of "paying attention" in relation to Greg's study in the next section.

Detecting and exploiting *subtexts* and *breakdowns*

In much focus group work (as in most research) the information gathered is just the tip of the iceberg and indexes additional information that would help researchers understand both participants' experiences and the conditions of those experiences in deeper, richer, more complete ways. But how do researchers know what is being indexed and how to access it? Detecting and following up on *subtexts* and *breakdowns* are especially useful in this process.

According to dictionary definitions, a subtext is an underlying, often hidden, theme in a text (e.g. conversation, poem, novel, play, photograph, film) or a message that is not directly stated but can usually be inferred or grasped through processes of contextualization and intertextualization. In artful texts, a subtext is often created to communicate principles, ideologies, or controversial issues and relationships that might put off readers and viewers if stated more directly. For example, a homoerotic relationship between Captain Kirk and Dr. Spock has often been claimed to be a subtext of the original television series, *Star Trek*, which was produced at a time when American television tended to avoid even implicit on-screen portrayals of sexual situations (especially non-traditional ones).

In the context of everyday life, *subtext* refers to the social fact that in real life people rarely say exactly what they mean but code those meanings in some way. For example, interlocutors often "beat around the bush" about or downplay their true beliefs, investments, feelings, or understandings about topics (especially emotionally charged topics). Their behavior in this regard is all the more heightened when they have some ambivalence toward a topic or have suffered pain or trauma in relation to it. Thus, both the interlocutor and the researcher must try to figure out the meanings not expressed—not what was said but what was really meant by what was said. In focus group research, this means remembering what seem to be subtexts in participants' talk and looking for openings to explore unsaid but implied meanings more fully.

Breakdowns also index implied or unsaid meanings and thus function in very similar ways in the research context. In his classic phenomenological treatise, *Being and Time*, Martin Heidegger (1962/1927) claimed that human understanding is not the layering of assertions onto experiences but an unpacking of the experiences itself. He also argued that the primary function of interpretation is to make explicit what is already within the range of human awareness, to make clearer what is already there. How one does this involves moving between three basic modes of being-in-the-world and the kinds of understanding each affords. These modes are the "ready-to-hand," the "unready-to-hand," and the "present-at-hand." The first two modes are most relevant for our purposes here. The "ready-to-hand" mode of understanding is non-reflective, engaged, embodied. The actor and the experience are one, and the actor does not really have to plan and think about what she is doing. Accomplished piano playing, cycling along a smooth oft-traveled road, a romantic partnership is rich and fulfilling, and being in the flow of writing are examples of this mode. The "unready-to-hand" mode is the *breakdown* mode. The pianist misses a note or loses the proper tempo. The cyclist encounters sand on the road or gets a flat tire. One of the partners in love becomes seriously ill. The writer loses her flow of ideas or is haunted by a previously written section she does not think works quite like she wants it to work. During these *breakdowns*, the actors are forced to be more reflective, more analytic. They "see" their field of practice (its elements, its tools, its actions, its purposes, its basic organization, its rules, etc.) more circumspectly, more fully, and more abstractly. And these new ways of seeing—insights—allow them to understand and often to remedy the *breakdown* they encountered.

As we noted in Chapter 2, Patti Lather and Chris Smithies (1997) encountered several kinds of *breakdowns* in their research with women living with HIV/AIDS. Group dynamics among these women were unpredictable, emotionally charged (even ravaging), and changed constantly across the project, forcing Lather and Smithies to constantly re-evaluate their understandings of their "data." In her "post book," Lather (2001, p. 210) acknowledged experiencing at least two emotional breakdowns as she bore witness to the women's experiences and stories that almost prevented her from being able to continue the work but that eventually allowed her to deepen her understandings of her participants and the exigencies of their lives. In relation to this point, Lather and Smithies end up celebrating what they call a "methodology of getting lost," a methodology built around the fundamental importance of detecting and exploiting *breakdowns*:

> At some level, the book is about getting lost across the various layers and registers, about not finding one's way into making a sense that maps easily onto our usual ways of making sense. Here we all get lost: the women, the researchers, the readers, the angels, in order to open up present frames of knowing to the possibilities of thinking differently.
>
> (Lather and Smithies, 1997, p. 52)

Indeed, listening for and responding to *subtexts* and to emotional, cognitive, and pragmatic *breakdowns* also opens up kinds and amounts of talk that are easily left behind unless researchers notice and ask about them. In George's study of new immigrant women, responding to *breakdowns* and *subtexts* turned out to be extremely important in a series of discussions about our participants' educational experiences and histories. Recall the segment of transcript in which Elana "confessed" to having a learning disability. The conversation in which this occurred began as a response to a question we asked our participants about their children's experiences in school. Little that seemed interesting or problematic emerged except for some frustration about speaking English well enough to talk productively with their children's teachers. When, however, the women were asked about their own school experiences, floodgates opened. Many women shared stories about both positive and negative experiences of schooling in Mexico. One woman (Elana) did not participate and seemed on the verge of tears. The topic of school experiences was revisited during the next few gatherings. Elana remained silent and continued to appear on the verge of tears. Then one evening, for reasons we can only speculate about, she revealed that she had a learning disability, that teachers and fellow students alike had called her "stupid" throughout school, that she still bore scars of shame from these experiences, and that she feared her children might suffer the same fate. In response, many other women shared even more powerful and painful stories of negative school experiences than they had shared during our first discussion of this general topic. Additionally, they engaged in conversations about various biological, psychological, and social structures and forces that can "damage" students. Finally, they shared strategies for protecting their own children against potentially negative school experiences.

Although they were different in character and played out in quite different ways, Greg experienced *breakdowns* in the focus groups devoted to discussions of *Panther* as well. As above, these breakdowns turned out to be instructive. More specifically, Greg and George attempted to lead several discussions of the film with these youth. But both the viewing and discussion groups often became (or at least we thought) wildly off topic. For example, participants often abandoned talk about *Panther* to discuss other films and the actors who played in them. The segment of talk showcased below took place at a point in the film that showed the police beating up a young black man. Because this segment is both brief and glib, understanding its full import requires considerable contextualization, which we offer up below:

S: They hitting the black man pretty hard!
T: They thumped him in the jaw!
(The actor who played Panther leader, Huey Newton, then entered the scene to confront the police.)
S: There go me!
T: I already called it!
S: That's my man!
T: Man, that's Ezell.
S: Where's Kane at?

First and foremost, we see once again a focus on the anti-police theme of the film. As noted earlier, this was a primary reason why the film was so widely embraced by the youth—it connected to real, ongoing issues in their lives. But more importantly, this segment of response highlights a common practice of our youth participants—to "call out" or "claim" characters as they watched films and television shows. Here, the character of Huey Newton, the leader of the Black Panther Party for Self Defense, is claimed by one of our participants as he confronts police. But there is something else about this practice (and our responses to it) that was absolutely critical in this study. This act of "claiming" led to a complex chained discussion of related films and the actors who played parts both in *Panther* and in these other films. Ezell is a character from the film *Friday*. He plays a "crack addict" in that film, and the fact that he played characters as different as Huey Newton and Ezell caught some of our young viewers off guard. "Kane"—a character from the film *Menace II Society*—is also mentioned. Both *Friday* and *Menace II Society* were wildly popular films, ones that were part of the mid-1990s bloom on hip hop scored films featuring rap icons highlighting everyday life in the "ghetto." Much of the energy and excitement generated while watching *Panther*, then, was connected to participants' affective investments in a whole constellation of films associated with hip hop culture. "Calling" or "claiming" characters indexed the deep investments these youth had in popular culture, broadly defined. Understanding this fact was absolutely essential for excavating the meaning and importance of the glib and fragmented bits of dialogue that constitute the transcript segment we shared above. The practice of "calling" or "claiming" also highlights the ways that focus groups can move in unpredictable directions and reveal unexpected connections, especially when researchers allow participants to engage in their own culturally informed reception practices. Part of the reason that *Panther* was taken up so dramatically was because it was connected in non-trivial ways to a genre of film with which these youth were invested. Had we censored their "calling" and "claiming"—which we were tempted to do because it seemed off task and resistant to us at first—we probably would not have come to understand much of the richness and complexity involved in these young people's understanding of and investments in popular culture.

The youth in this study also forged other kinds of unpredictable (again, to us) connections between and among a variety of popular cultural forms. For example, as illustrated in the transcript segment below, several youth were talking about some recent schoolyard fights they had been in. Their conversation was elliptical and confusing so Greg asked what they were talking about and why. They responded as follows:

S: See the dude had hit my sister and I got up and hit 'em. My sister don't like to fight, I said "why you didn't hit 'em back" and she said "it didn't hurt," so I went over there and hit 'em.

G: Why are you all into it?

S: 'Cause we help each other. We the Black Panthers. We NOW. NOW 4 Life!

The last sentence, "'Cause we help each other. We the Black Panthers. We NOW. NOW 4 Life!" is key to understanding what is going on here. NOW was a professional wrestling team, popular when this research was being conducted.

These youth forged connections among their own social networks ("we help each others"), the Panthers ("We the Black Panthers"), and professional wrestling ("We NOW"). These connections were quite interesting and went a long way to understanding how and why *Panther* (as opposed to the other films) was taken up so readily. But at the time, we didn't understand the connections the youth were making. Instead, we saw them as distractions, digressions, and tangents. There were even some moments during the film when the youth tried out wrestling moves on each other as opposed to watching the film (these were typically during the talking parts). We were flummoxed. These were *breakdowns* in the research process for us. We worried that we were not getting and never would get the data we needed to fully understand these young people's investments in popular culture. Ironically, though, we were getting just that. We just didn't realize it. In retrospect, our participants were telling us why this film connected so powerfully in their lives, as well as how many other popular cultural resources functioned in similar ways and—most importantly—how all of their investments were connected in cohesive powerful ways that we could neither see nor imagine. Although we cannot be sure, we really doubt that these connections and insights would have emerged for us had we only conducted observations and individual interviews at the community center. Utilizing focus groups—and especially noticing and following up on *subtexts* and *breakdowns* during focus group activity—rendered what was invisible to us visible and allowed us to understand the depth and complexity of our participants' investments in multiple forms of popular culture, as well as the *hows* and *whys* that grounded these investments.

In addition, these responses highlight the importance of "paying attention to and following up" on participants' comments as noted in the previous section. For example, Greg actively intervened in the above discussion around schoolyard fights, asking the young participants to explain how and why they got into the fights they did. Their comments about the Panthers and NOW—a connection we would have otherwise missed—emerged in their responses to his query. Among other things, this example highlights the fact that *subtexts* and *breakdown* are not always readily visible. Paying careful attention to what is said and following up appropriately is key in this regard.

If we think about the *subtexts* and *breakdowns* that occurred in the two studies showcased in this chapter, another interesting element of focus group work comes into view. Both the participants and the facilitators can be the ones who experience *breakdowns*. In the study of new immigrant women, Elana (a participant) had an emotional *breakdown* that opened up new avenues for understanding. In the study of urban young people's investments in popular culture, both because of cultural differences and their own agendas, Greg and George experienced a *breakdown* in seeing and understanding connections that were patently obvious to their participants.

Our primary claim in this section has been that *subtexts* and *breakdowns* often signal extremely important knowledge that motivate people's behaviors and investments, as well as structures and forces in their lives that contribute to their problems and oppression but that they are reluctant to share for many reasons, often to save face. Being aware that this is the case, detecting and gently pursuing what seem to be *subtexts*, and responding effectively to *breakdowns* quite often results in very rich data indeed (usually highly contextualized stories that index meso-level and macro-level social, cultural, political, and economic structures and forces that exert powerful [usually negative] effects on participants' lives).

Creating opportunities for building solidarity and political synergy

We discussed some of the ways in which building solidarity and igniting political synergy in the context of focus group work often leads to transformative outcomes. For example, we noted that the consciousness raising groups (CRGs) of second- and third-wave feminism were deployed to mobilize empowerment agendas and to enact social change, and that they set the scene for the political function of focus group work. We also unpacked some of the ways in which the work of Esther Madriz (especially 2000) built upon and extended earlier feminist, anti-oppressive research around the constructs/practices of collective engagement, testimony, and voice. Finally, we provided examples of the ways in which other feminist researchers (e.g. Dorinne Kondo, Smadar Lavie, Ruth Behar, Aiwa Ong, and Lila Abu-Lughod) have focused on the affordances of solidarity building and political synergy in their research, as well as how CAR and PAR have further expanded the purview of politically-inflected forms of focus group research.

Indeed, creating opportunities for building solidarity among participants is crucial to focus group work, and when researchers are successful in this regard, solidarity very often leads to political synergy and effective social activist work. In this section, we share some of the strategies we have used for creating opportunities for building solidarity in our focus group work, as well as some of the successful social activist work that participants in solidarity have accomplished.

In all of our studies, we have tried to create opportunities where participants could mingle, share experiences, and develop friendships. During these "down times," participants often galvanized around shared issues and problems, and their shared experiences and commitments often laid foundations for collective social and political action. The transcript segments about English language learning, healthcare, and transportation we have shared throughout this chapter from the study of new immigrant women have all embodied evidence of emerging solidarity relations and indexed the activist orientations latent in such relations. For example, recall that the women engaged in many discussions about how frustrating many aspects of their lives were because they didn't speak English well. These were mostly "gripe" sessions with little talk about how the women might function as change agents in relation to this problem. As the women were encouraged to reflect more deeply on this problem, an increasing sense of trust and urgency developed among them, which eventually surfaced some hidden, macro-level factors such as linguistic and cultural imperialism. The focus groups also generated considerable political synergy around discontents with the opportunities for English language learning in the community, as well as the negative consequences for the women of not having access to high quality instructors and instruction.

Largely as a function of focus group conversations we have discussed in this chapter, the women in the new immigrant study (as well as other Latinas in the community) engaged in a variety of concrete activist activities that resulted in improvements in ESL instruction and healthcare access and quality for the Latino community. For example, the women wrote a "manifesto" that listed all of the elements they believed ought to be included in English language learning classes for adults. These elements ranged from having classes at times when working parents could attend to financial aid to childcare to conversation-focused instruction to high quality teachers to providing amnesty for undocumented citizens. They also lobbied the Latino Coalition and other agencies to push for more translators in hospitals and clinics. They composed a letter to the editor of the local newspaper about the need for translation services in these sites. And they assembled and distributed an information sheet about the documentation required to open checking and savings accounts at most local banks and credit unions. Finally, they composed a bilingual flyer expressing the need for healthcare agencies to better promote their services within the Latino community and to communicate with clients in Spanish, and they enlisted the help of the Latino Coalition to distribute them throughout the community. Within two years, and largely motivated by this focus group work, many positive changes occurred in the community. The nature and scope of ESL classes available in the community changed considerably and along the lines suggested. The Industrial Federal Credit Union hired five bilingual tellers.

With respect to mobility and problems with reliable and affordable transportation, the women wasted no time in taking action to better the conditions of their lives. Within weeks after these issues were put squarely on the table, the women created a co-op ride sharing system. This system grew and became very efficient over time. Besides serving the women's transportation needs quite well, this co-op forced mercenary car services to lower their fees. Additionally, over the course of about a year, women who had licenses began to teach women who didn't how to drive and arranged for them to take their driving tests.

Looking across these various activities motivated largely by our focus group work, a complex set of interrelated marginalizing forces become visible, as well as the ways in which the women in the study "talked back" (hooks, 1989) to these forces. Latinas who did not work also did not know how to drive. Their English proficiency was low, but they did not take English classes for a variety of reasons. Their husbands controlled their access to mobility and educational opportunities, which meant they had difficulty going to events like parent teacher conferences and, more generally, fulfilling their many responsibilities for generations above and below them. These various forces of oppression were related to each other and to larger forces operating both within and outside of the Mexican American community. Participating in focus group work helped these women begin to see these patterns and the relations between and among them. Once these patterns were visible and once considerable solidarity was established, they began to develop strategies for working against the structures and forces preventing them to live the kinds of lives they hoped to live. And, in many respects, their activist efforts were very successful.

Greg's RAPPS study also enabled some interesting political activities. While the focus groups for this study were being conducted, the Ku Klux Klan proposed a rally in the small city where the community center was located and our participants lived. Fears of the Klan were paramount in this community, and many young people shared stories—real and apocryphal—of the group's terrorist acts. Many of these stories were family stories, including experiences that relatives or friends had had with the Klan in the South. Clearly, this was a collective history that ran deep, making the prospect of the rally deeply unsettling. Some of the youth were afraid that the Klan would follow them in the streets, come to their homes, or hurt their families. Interestingly, much of the informal talk at the club turned to how the Panthers might have responded to this kind of threat. Comments like "We need the Panthers here!" were tossed around. Clearly, the history of the Klan's violence within African American community struck close to home, was experienced viscerally, and resonated deeply with the young people in the study. In facing their fears, they did not turn to the histories they learned in school to make sense of things. Instead, they turned to a popular cultural text with which they resonated as a group. They turned to *Panther*, and they used much of the knowledge about the film they had learned during focus group conversations to cope with their fear and dread.

In both of the studies we have discussed in this chapter, the power of focus groups to generate understandings that have personal and collective relevance— knowledge that is vital, useful, and communally shared—has been a salient theme. Additionally, we have seen some of the ways that this knowledge can and does mobilize effective personal, social and political work.

Conclusions

Our accounts of some of the key principles or strategies for successful focus group work show the contingent and unpredictable potential for linkages among inquiry, politics, and pedagogy that is always latent in focus group work. This potential often discloses complexities, nuances, and contradictions embodied in "lived experience." It indexes social and economic forces such as linguistic imperialism, economic exploitation, racism, and sexism that often get glossed over or explained away by one or another cultural logic. It also indexes connections among apparently disparate activity systems (e.g. hip hop culture, gangs, and the World Wrestling Federation) that are invisible to all but "cultural insiders." These positive outcomes are, of course, accompanied by attendant dangers. Given how power operates within relations of dominance and oppression, for example, naming and talking back to imperialism or sexism can have serious, even devastating, consequences. Indeed, the participants in the immigrant women project faced such consequences in their marriages, in the Mexican American community, in the workplace, and in the community at large. Although participants in the popular culture study did not face negative consequences for their participation (or at least any of which we are aware), there was some consternation among the senior staff about what they were doing and learning. For example, there was some concern early on that we were discussing things like gang activity without a clear pedagogical or interventionist agenda. Concerns were also expressed about the fact that we were collecting potentially incriminating material about our participants that might some time, somehow, and in some way be used against them. Because it is dynamic, multifaceted, and unpredictable, focus group work never comes with guarantees. Both positive and negative outcomes are possible, and researchers need to modulate these possible outcomes situationally and in the best ways they know how.

This issue notwithstanding, the unique potentials of focus group research are most fully realized when we acknowledge and exploit their multiple functions. To return to the metaphor with which we opened this chapter, the multifunctionality of focus group work is usefully imagined as a prism. That is, the three sides of this prism—pedagogy, politics, and research—are always implicated in and productive of each other. One surface of the prism may be most visible at any particular moment, but the others are always also visible, refracting what is brought to light in multiple and complex directions. How we choose to "hold" this imaginary prism at any moment in time has important consequences both for what we see and what we do with what we see.

Chapter 5

Contemporary dilemmas and horizons of focus group research

We have attempted in this book to develop a more expansive understanding of the nature, functions, and affordances of focus groups and focus group work than currently exists in the extant, extensive literature on this general topic. In doing so, we have chronicled the history of focus group research within applied disciplines, as well as its multiple origins outside of areas traditionally associated with empirical research (e.g. the literacy circles of Paulo Freire). We have looked at the ways attending to the specificity of focus group work allows us to develop new conceptual categories to analyze and understand our empirical material. Although this book has been primarily conceptual, we reject the notion that conceptual work can easily be distinguished from the gritty practicalities of research in the field. Because the two are always of a piece, we have interleaved practical advice for researchers and real world examples throughout the book. Importantly, this material has not been added on in an *ad hoc* fashion. Rather, we have tried to demonstrate how and to explain why the conceptual and the practical are always inextricably intertwined. We extend this impulse to twin the conceptual and practical in this final chapter as we look at contemporary threats to—and future possibilities for—focus group work.

Key here are the analytic categories particular to this work. As we noted in Chapter 2, focus group work performs three primary functions (often simultaneously): inquiry, pedagogy, and political action. As we illustrated in Chapter 3, focus group work has some quasi-unique affordances. These include: mitigating the researcher's authority and generating deeper understandings; disclosing the constitutive power of discourse and the lifeblood of social activity; approximating the natural; filling in knowledge gaps and saturating understanding; drawing out complexity, nuance, and contradiction; disclosing eclipsed or invisible connections; and creating opportunities for solidarity building and political action. Because of the quasi-unique affordances, particular rich, complex, and nuanced kinds of data often emerge from focus groups that seldom emerge from other data collection strategies including observations and one-on-one interviews. Additionally, particular understandings of self are drawn out in focus group work that are different from those drawn out in individual interviews—selves-in-dialogue, social selves, selves-in-community. And in Chapter 4, we shared what we believe are essential elements for conducting dialogic, synergistic focus groups. These include: expecting, even celebrating, unpredictable group dynamics, conflict, and contradiction; exploiting pre-existing social networks that encourage collegiality; creating safe, comfortable, and even festive spaces "of" the people; using open-ended prompts for questions and then letting group participants direct the flow of talk and interaction; keeping notes and following up on key themes and gaps; listening for *breakdowns* and *subtexts* and asking for elaboration; and trying to create openings for social solidarity and political synergy.

In this chapter, we deploy these ideas as pivots to animate and re-animate discussions about pressing contemporary issues in qualitative inquiry (generally) and focus group work (specifically). These include: contemporary threats to focus group work and strategic responses to these threats; research ethics and the public/private split; and problems and possibilities for focus group work in Web 2.0. In relation to each of these issues, we show how attending to the specific functions and affordances of focus group research allow new angles of vision for the potentials for focus group research today.

Contemporary threats to focus group work and strategic responses to these threats

Institutional Review Boards (IRBs) are university and college committees that oversee the protection of all individuals or "subjects" participating in research by university personnel (in the United States). These committees must insure that all such research is compliant with the principles and policies of the federal government (more on this below). By legal obligation, they are required for all colleges and universities that receive federal funding. Although primarily targeted towards research funded by federal grants, most universities and colleges require all faculty members and students to comply with their guidelines and principles. Ostensibly, IRB policies signal a general concern with the well being and protection of all human subjects. However, some argue that universities have begun to use these policies to protect against and derail potential lawsuits (e.g. Christians, 2011, p. 67).

Interestingly, many professional organizations had already developed codes of ethics similar to those of IRBs during the twentieth century. The central role of the US federal government only became pronounced in 1978 with the publication of the *Belmont Report: Ethical Principles and Guidelines for the Protection of Human Subjects of Research (Report of the National Commission for the Protection of Human Subjects of Biomedical and Behavioral Research)*. This report came in response to past abuses of federally funded research including the Tuskegee Syphilis Study where researchers knowingly left poor black men who had the disease untreated to observe its "evolution" over time. The report focused on three moral standards for research with human subjects. These were (a) respect for persons or the principle that individuals be treated as autonomous agents entering into the research voluntarily; (b) beneficence or the idea that individuals should be protected from harm in the research while maximizing benefits to individuals and others; and (c) justice or the idea that no individual or group is unduly burdened and rewards and benefits are distributed equally to all participants. As is obvious, the *Belmont Report* was a response to and focused on biomedical and behavioral research. In time, though, its principles were brought to bear on all of the natural and social sciences. Additionally, residues of the original purposes for the *Belmont Report* persist. To this day, IRBs are often made up of medical and behavioral scientists who, for the most part, conduct experimental research and know little about the assumptions, practices, and purposes of qualitative research. In other words, to these scientists the only kind of research with which they are really knowledgeable about is research that has clear inputs and outputs and is conducted in controlled settings (e.g. randomized field trials). Their ability to fairly evaluate risks to human subjects in more naturalistic research studies has been the subject of ongoing debates for decades now.

One central concern of these debates has been about the question/issue of "anonymity," which we will use here to discuss the more general issue of "threats to focus group work and strategic responses to those threats." The basic concern with "respect for persons" often means a concern with protecting the integrity of participants including their right to be anonymous in public presentations of research. At the very least, participants should not face negative repercussions for their roles in research projects. Using pseudonyms and eliminating all identity markers in data sets are the typical ways the identities of research subjects are protected. Researchers are usually required to provide detailed plans by which they will protect the identities of the people with whom they work and to keep secure the material they gather. It is not uncommon for IRBs to request that interview data be recorded using pseudonyms and that all data be password protected on encrypted files.

The very public nature of focus groups problematizes the issue of anonymity, as well as the theories of self upon which the very idea of anonymity is grounded. By their nature, focus groups generate public data—or at least data that are more public than one-on-one interviews. As we have pointed out throughout this book, the fact that focus groups are socially intense is a primary reason for their unique power in getting at the *hows* and *whys* of whatever is being studied. As we demonstrated in our discussions of Freire's study circles and the feminist collectives of the 1970s, individuals engaged in dialogue generate insights and information that seldom are generated during observations of naturally occurring activity or in one-on-one interviews. In fact, as we have argued throughout, focus groups should indeed be conceptualized as *groups* and not simply as collections of individuals. This means that the most appropriate unit of analysis for focus group work is the collective. This conceptual/operational shift raises some practical concerns about safeguarding the anonymity of individuals within groups. Some examples will help here.

Greg has served as major advisor and committee member for doctoral students who used focus groups as a primary tool for collecting empirical material. One student, Getnet Tizazu Fetene, mentioned above, studied attitudes towards HIV/AIDS among college-aged youth in Ethiopia. This project was flagged by the university IRB as potentially "high risk" endeavors, even though both students had been proactive in arguing that these very commonly discussed topics were not likely to cause undue stress among participants. Still, the question of anonymity remained central among the IRB's concerns. Although these students' proposals all stated clearly that they would require strict confidentiality among participants, there was no real way to guarantee this. After all, anyone in the group could elect to speak about whatever he or she wished to whomever—including information about sensitive, highly charged, personal topics. If someone, for instance, revealed some personal aspect of their sex life to Getnet, the participant could ask later to have those revelations removed from the data set and never used in public presentations of the research. Anyone in the group, however, could use the information as they wished. As a result of this, some members of the IRB suggested doing large numbers of one-on-one interviews instead of conducting focus groups.

What was really at issue became clearer when Greg talked with the IRB. Unfamiliar with focus group work, some members thought focus groups were simply used to conduct multiple interviews simultaneously—as a time saving measure. Although these understandings reflected unfamiliarity with focus group research, they also echoed several vestigial elements from the history of focus group research that we discussed in Chapter 1. Recall, for example, that the earliest proponents of focus group work stressed that "focus" could allow for a larger number of people to be interviewed simultaneously. That is, focus groups were an efficient way to conduct research. Recall also that this time saving aspect of focus group work was picked up in commercial industries, as well as in professional and applied fields. But members of IRBs typically do not know this history (or any of the histories of method development within qualitative research for that matter). Nor are they concerned with saving the researcher time and effort. Why should they be? Because the IRB members who reviewed Getnet's proposal did not understand the logics, functions, and affordances of focus group work, they flagged their use as a problem with the research design that needed to be addressed.

On behalf of Getnet, Greg met with the IRB and provided historical and conceptual information about focus groups relevant to their concerns—including the fact that participants often feel more comfortable talking about sensitive topics in peer groups because this setting diminishes personal vulnerability and risk. He also explained (with convincing examples from the qualitative research methods literature) that some kinds of information are more likely to be shared in focus group discussions (including and perhaps especially information about sex and sexuality) that would almost never be shared in one-on-one interviews. In effect, he used several of the arguments we have discussed in this book—such as how focus groups allow participants safe spaces for talk and social interaction, invoke collective experience and memory, create opportunities for solidarity building, and motivate collective political synergy to make his arguments. As we emphasized in Chapter 3, these affordances seldom emerge in one-on-one interviews, where the interviewer has more authority and holds more discursive control of the setting and process of information gathering. In short, Greg provided evidence-based arguments for how and why focus groups yield richer, more accurate social science data than individual interviews. In doing so, he used language and concepts that were familiar to typical IRB members and that, in a sense, co-opted their concerns. The IRB found his arguments compelling and approved the proposals.

The validity of Greg's arguments were clearly borne out in Getnet's study. Participants supported and responded to each other in very productive ways in their focus group conversations. Although AIDS was considered a very sensitive topic by the IRB (for good reasons, of course), participants clearly indicated that it was a topic with which they were deeply familiar and thus one that people of their generation neither needed to nor wanted to discuss—a point that we discussed at length in Chapter 3. Finally, Getnet's study brought into high relief the fact that the *collective* is the most appropriate unit of analysis for focus group work, as well as the fact that anonymity is a problematic construct when selves are theorized as selves-with-others, social selves, selves-in-community.

Indeed, participants in Getnet's study formed a contingent, collective identity—challenging the notion that they did not "know" about HIV/AIDS. They constantly built upon and extended each other's knowledge and experiences ("I think this is the overall feeling here") and lodged a far-reaching group critique of HIV/AIDS education programs in Ethiopia. The synergy that developed among his participants reinforced Getnet's orientation to research, the orientation advocated in this book. They took ownership of discussions and used them for their own purposes. Because the knowledge produced in the focus group sessions was largely an effect of the social synergy that developed among participants, it seems highly unlikely that similar data would have emerged had Getnet conducted many one-on-one interviews as the IRB had originally suggested.

To put it differently, Greg had to argue for the practical and theoretical specificity of focus group work. As detailed throughout this book, focus groups are not simply extensions of one-on-one interviews. They have their own specificity and autonomy. This needed to be made explicit to IRB members. Although the question of anonymity remained a thorny one to the IRB, it was reconstructed (and thus resolved) in the following way: the potential risk of participants breaking anonymity in focus groups was outweighed by the valuable information that could only be generated from group discussions. What is most important for our purposes here is the fact that getting approval for this research required educating powerful administrators about the benefits of a data collection strategy about which they had almost no knowledge. They knew nothing about the history of using focus groups in research, and they had little familiarity with its unique functions and affordances.

Our discussion of this experience with this IRB is worth underscoring. As is well documented, IRBs can be problematic gatekeepers for qualitative researchers because, by and large, they still operate from within a positivist epistemological orientation and evaluate all research against the standard of the medical model.

Unmarked research for them is research that has individual subjects, large Ns, control groups, isolated variables, and clearly delimited interventions. Moreover, ethically grounded in the *Belmont Report*, they are fundamentally concerned with assessing the tensions and tradeoffs of means-end/risk-reward ratios. These logics and concerns can be appropriated and re-inflected by qualitative researchers to argue for research that is equally legitimate but less familiar to IRB members. In the case we just discussed, Greg did just this in relation to the issue of anonymity. In the current political climate—perhaps more than ever before—researchers need to educate IRBs about how the potential benefits of unfamiliar data collection strategies outweigh their potential risks.

Research ethics and the public/private split

An even more vexing conceptual issue is indexed by Greg's experience with the IRB at his institution. IRBs function to protect individual "subjects." However, one argument we have made throughout this book is that the most appropriate unit of analysis for much qualitative research is not individual but the group. In many respects, this shift provides a challenge to how guidelines for the ethical conduct of research are constructed. So, it would be useful to step back a bit here and talk about the philosophical and institutional foundations upon which IRBs rest.

As Cliff Christians (2011) has argued, the history of ethical deliberations about research in the West has been grounded in the Enlightenment tradition since the seventeenth century. This tradition privileges value neutrality, individual autonomy, and utilitarian means-ends calculations. Within this tradition, ethical guidelines are generated outside of particular communities and operationalized as a series of disconnected rules to be applied in cookie-cutter fashion. The individual remains the unit of analysis here, marginalizing the role and importance of community in the generation and application of ethical standards; similarly, these kinds of means-ends ratios are created to balance potential risks and benefits to individuals (and ultimately the public). These logics—all of which are rooted in the Enlightenment tradition—are ones that Christians and others see as increasingly unable to address the ethical challenges of our current historical moment. Even more troubling is the fact that IRBs currently function more to protect institutions from lawsuits than to protect individuals from physical or psychological harm (e.g. Christians, 2011; Denzin and Lincoln, 2005, 2011).

Christians (2011) also highlighted the particular limitations of current IRB policies and practices for thinking about the privacy of the individual. "Codes and ethics," he noted, "insist on safeguards to protect people's identities and those of the research locations. Confidentiality must be assured as the primary safeguard against unwanted exposure" (p. 66). Such safeguards are built upon the assumption of the autonomous self, a problematic legacy Enlightenment thinking, where the "self became essential to the construction of a unique personhood" (p. 66). This conception of the self precludes other more social, communal, and democratic conceptions of the self. "Democratic life was articulated outside these atomistic units, a secondary domain of negotiated contracts and problematic communication" (p. 66). This version of individual autonomy has proven difficult to sustain today. "Despite the signature status of privacy protection, watertight confidentiality has proven to be impossible . . . Encoding privacy protection is meaningless when there is no distinction between the public and private that has consensus any longer" (p. 66).

In the face of this dilemma, Christians has proposed another form of ethics—one that:

> presumes the community is ontologically and axiologically prior to people. Human identity is constituted through the social realm, and human bonding is the epicenter of social formation. We are born into a sociological universe where values, moral commitments, and existential meanings are negotiated dialogically.
>
> (Christians, 2011, p. 70)

This form of ethics is ground zero for focus groups research as we have described it in this book. And the most appropriate unit of analysis for such an ethics is the group and not the individual. Among other things, this epistemological orientation opens up possibilities for emergent group norms becoming the basis for new forms of ethics.

Christians' ruminations about the ethics of research echo a recent and very powerful trajectory of thought in cultural historical activity theory built upon the work of Mikhail Bakhtin, especially his philosophical anthropology. Bakhtin has long been appropriated by social science scholars primarily to think about the dialogic nature of discourse. Indeed, his theories of the "utterance," "heteroglossia," "social languages," and "speech genres" have been widely taken up and applied. His dialogic theories of the self—which are predicated on the same basic principles as his dialogic theories of language and discourse—have received much less attention but are particularly relevant here.

According to Bakhtin (1990, 1993), individuals develop within unique histories that are ethically motivated. Dialogue—both with concrete others and with social discourses—is fundamentally a matter of answerability or being ethically responsive within social relationships. Individual selves develop in response to specific others and affiliations with collectives through relationships of care, empathy, and ethical responsibility. How individual selves appropriate socially shared texts and practices—the dimension of Bakhtin's work most commonly discussed—always and only happens within meaningful engagements with specific others. Any philosophical anthropology, Bakhtin argued, must pivot on the real histories of real individuals engaged in relations of "answerability" wherein each individual "owns" her responses to others and "intones" them with both her own meanings and those compelled by the other in dialogue. This claim was predicated on his insistence that the other is essential to the formation of the self—the individual's "absolute need for the other, for the other's seeing, remembering, gathering, and unifying self-activity" (Bakhtin, 1990, pp. 35–36). And for Bakhtin, this need has affective, valuational, and cognitive dimensions. How the self develops in and through its relationships with other selves always involves care, compassion, mutual responsibility, and love.

Crucial for our purposes here is that Bakhtin insisted that such a practical philosophical anthropology could never be adequately constructed in relation to any form of Enlightenment ethics. Bakhtin saw chains of caring and ethical answerability as fundamental to social life and social justice. Without attention to its emotional-volitional dimensions, human intercourse becomes susceptible to rationalist objectification. It loses what makes it qualitatively different from the more objective, determinate kinds of relations that constitute the natural world. Only within relationships of answerability can individuals (with others) embrace or resist the historical or cultural realities in which they find themselves. Reason is most rational when one is morally and ethically answerable to oneself and to others. "The actually performed act in its undivided wholeness is more than rational—it is *answerable*. Rationality is but a moment of answerability . . . like the glimmer of a lamp before the sun" (Bakhtin, 1993, p. 29).

Living a meaningful, ethically responsible life then means living responsively with others, which is largely a matter of paying attention to and being willing to be moved to action by the particulars of others' actions, feelings, thoughts, and evaluative responses. "Life can be consciously comprehended only in concrete answerability. . . . A life that has fallen away from answerability cannot have a philosophy; it is, in its very principle, fortuitous and incapable of being rooted" (Bakhtin, 1993, p. 56). From the points of view of Bakhtin's dialogic philosophical anthropology—and the theory and research it has spawned in the human sciences—conceptions of ethics that motivate the policies and practices of IRBs seem woefully inadequate indeed. It is high time to develop new conceptions—ones that take seriously the ways in which the self is always already social.

Like the work of Christians and recent invocations of Bakhtin's philosophical anthropology within social scientific theories of the self, focus groups and focus group research have motivated the need for rethinking the constructs of "public" and "private," as well as the consequences of operating with particular versions of such constructs. In many respects, focus groups are "public" sources of data collection. They are certainly more public than one-on-one interviews and even more public than observations. As such, they constitute new ways to think about emergent public spheres. While participants can speak with/as a public voice in their interactions with others in focus conversations, focus groups are often also "safe spaces" for participants. And this idea of safe spaces invokes a sense of the private—spaces that are small and intimate where personal issues may be shared with a personally chosen, select group of others. In this respect, focus groups can serve as key sites for re-imagining how private and public can be understood, mediated, and negotiated.

This point is worth underscoring. Politics has traditionally assumed a split between private and public spheres. The public sphere has been assumed the realm of "official politics" where one leaves one's private interests, assumptions, and biases behind. The "public voice" in politics is logical and designed for collective persuasion (e.g. Levine, 2008). Drawing on Amy Gutmann and Dennis Thompson's (1996) work, Levine argued that "[w]hen in the public sphere, one must advance arguments that any rational person can accept. That means that one may not express arbitrary opinions, assert purely selfish interests, or appeal to authorities—such as Scripture—that others reject" (p. 120). The public figure is an "ethical and rational legislator, addressing an assembly of peers on matters of public concern" (p. 121).

Focus groups—as we have (re)defined them in this book—are extraordinarily fertile sites for rethinking this public/private split. Paradoxically, they are public spheres of potential collective action, but they do not ask us to leave behind the personal. In fact, focus groups are spaces where the personal can (and often does) become political. Recall here that this basic impulse was fundamental to the consciousness raising groups of second- and third-wave feminism and the study circles of Paulo Freire's *Pedagogy of the Oppressed*. Like those social movements, focus groups challenge normative notions of ethics grounded in Enlightenment notions of the self and the relations between the self and the social.

As such, focus groups can help us re-imagine aspects of the *Belmont Report* principles using the group (rather than the individual) as an organizing trope. Instead of worrying about the non-coercion of the individual, for example, what if we shifted our concerns to the non-coercion of groups as the central ethical issue? That is, how are different groups situated differently to participate in research or not? At what level is participation a personal decision or a collective one or both? Instead of thinking about individual risks and rewards, what if we thought about collective risks and rewards? How might we push discussions about research risks and rewards to encompass the ways different groups have been put in harms way? Or have benefited from research? Or have not benefited? Finally, how might we think about justice not so much in terms of the rights and freedoms of individuals but as social justice or the rights and freedoms of collectives—from groups defined by shared interests or experiences to social categories (e.g. groups constituted by race, class, gender, etc.)? What would it mean to fully embrace the idea that justice is a collective ideal? These are just a few of the questions we might want to ask if the *group* rather than the *individual* were the "unit of analysis" we used to ground research ethics.

We would like to make one final point about the question of anonymity in research. IRBs have traditionally been concerned about protecting the identities of individuals. We find it anomalous—and telling—that the participants in all of our focus group studies have often wanted their identities made public. Some have wanted this for the social capital and prestige it brought them in their peer groups (as with Greg's participants in *Friendship, Cliques, and Gangs*). Others have wanted this because it brought status and prestige to the group in relation to the larger community (as in the art groups Greg worked with for *Critical Dispositions* or the group of new immigrant women in George's study). In short, for both individuals and groups, anonymity is often low on their list of concerns—trumped by the desire for and prestige of public recognition. We might speculate why this is the case, invoking constructs like the conversationalization of public discourse (e.g. Fairclough, 1995) or new media forms such as talk shows, Facebook, Twitter, and so on. These speculations notwithstanding, a reconfigured approach to research ethics would put the problems and concerns we have raised here more squarely on the table.

Online focus groups

The modulation of the public and the private is at the heart of emerging Web 2.0 technologies. As such, we can reflect upon some of the issues being raised about Internet research through the conceptual tools of focus groups as discussed throughout this book. But before we begin, we should take stock of some of the current work on online focus groups. Even a cursory review of the literature shows that there is a lot of interest in online focus groups and their potentials. As Marilyn Lichtman (2011) noted in *Qualitative Research in Education: A User's Guide*,

> as the Internet becomes more widely available and as high speed connections link many people to the web and potentially to each other, conducting focus groups online offers a new alternative to the traditional type of focus group setting . . . I believe there is great potential for online focus groups. It is too early to say what methodological issues may arise.
>
> (p. 159)

Lichtman went on to suggest some concrete new possibilities for focus group work while also acknowledging that online focus groups constitute a wide-open terrain for possibilities not yet even imagined.

The nature and effects of differences between asynchronous and synchronous discussions—those that happen in "real time" and those that do not—are issues that have been addressed by many scholars. Among other things, these scholars have noted that asynchronous discussions are akin to listservs, blogs, or email discussion threads, and that synchronous discussions are more like instant messaging or other chat group formats where conversations unfolded in real time. Given these analogies, many of the concerns raised by these scholars—especially in applied fields such as marketing and health—have centered largely on the practicality of different kinds of discussion venues. In this regard, Brüggen and Willems (2009) emphasized that "the boom in online marketing research" is one of the "fastest growing" research segments in the field. The authors highlighted the advantages of online work, including "shorter project lead times, shorter field times, greater access to busy professionals, and international reach" (pp. 363–364). The same journal, Tuckel and Wood (2009) reported on a study of respondent cooperation in both conventional (face-to-face) and online focus group discussions. Here, too, the authors noted the growth of computer-mediated communication and its potential uses for marketing research. They also addressed the issue of how anonymity played out in the two conditions. In the end, the authors suggested that computer-mediated communication (CMC) may allow participants to interact more freely. Yet "the visual anonymity provided by CMC may lead to deindividuation," prompting "anti-normative behavior" such as "flaming." They went onto say that CMC group members may "feel freer to find fault with others' ideas, leading to more disagreement and criticism." At the same time, "the visual anonymity provided by CMC can lead to lowered self-awareness (as others cannot see you) and heightened private self-awareness (as one can reflect on one's own thoughts and how to type them), leading to increased self-disclosure" (p. 134).

Fox, Morris, and Rumsey (2007) discussed the implications of online focus group work for health research. In particular, they explored the use of online focus groups for drawing together participants with visible skin ailments. Here, too, questions of anonymity were paramount. They were particularly interested in the potential consequences of bringing together people who might be self-conscious about their appearance. Still, the authors voiced familiar enthusiasm for the practicality of online focus groups, "including reduced time and cost in terms of venues and traveling. It is also beneficial in eliminating transcription time and error" (p. 545).

In another article, Stewart and Williams (2007) compared online focus groups to "3D graphical environments" such as *Second Life*. They noted that "[f]eatures of Internet interactions such as perceived anonymity, reduced social cues, and the realization of time-space distanciation may lead individuals to reveal more about themselves within online environments than would be done in offline equivalents" (p. 399). They also suggested that users may perceive "computer mediated interactions as somewhat ephemeral: unguarded 'conversations on a train' in an uncensored unpoliced environment" (p. 399). The question of the importance of capturing and analyzing multiple social cues was extended in their comparisons between online focus groups and 3D, virtual reality environments. Here, the focus group setting is extended visually, allowing for a seemingly wider range of social cues and interactions. In this regard, the authors argued that

> some of the concerns that have plagued Internet research, such as the lack of proximal (use of space) and kinesical (body movement) features that aid in interpretation and analysis in offline setting, are now being nullified by these new and emerging 'physical' online environments.
>
> (Stewart and Williams, 2007, p. 407)

The rush to online focus groups has raised several interesting and important questions. For example, the idea that virtual reality environments might "nullify" the concerns of earlier work typifies the utopic thinking that often accompanies discussions of computer-mediated social spaces. One is reminded here of the fantasies that accompanied distance education—that it would be just as good as "the real thing." Yet, as many have come to realize, the communicative functions of the subtleties of bodily cues and other non-verbal elements of face-to-face interaction are not so easily re-created in virtual reality environments. Whether and to what extent the limitations of online focus groups are "nullified" within virtual reality environments thus remains an open question.

Utopian thinking is evident even in the language of most articles about the interactional and communicative affordances of new information technologies. Face-to-face interactions are even subtly recast as happening "offline"—as if the default were otherwise. Utopian impulses notwithstanding, all of these articles also insist that to understand the logics and affordances of online focus group work in richer, more sophisticated ways will require much more conceptual and empirical work.

Indeed, one great outcome of the advent of social media and other kinds of CMC is that they force us to engage with persistent questions on fresh terrain. At the very least, this means acknowledging that moving from face-to-face to technologically mediated forms of communication means moving into communicative domains that may be radically different from domains with which we are currently familiar and perhaps very different from each other as well. Each might be usefully thought of as a particular "modality" of interaction and communication with its own unique enablements and constraints. Questions that emerge from having multiple new modalities of interaction and communication available to us include the following: Can technologically mediated forms of communication draw out the complexities and nuances encountered in face-to-face communication? How might online interactions allow for groups to "take over" in ways that mitigate the role of the researcher even more than we have discussed in this book? What might *subtexts* and *breakdowns* look like within these new modalities? Whether and how might they motivate the radical modes of self-interrogation that can (and often do) happen in traditional focus group conversations? What else might they spawn? Answers to these (and similar) questions partially depend upon how we conceptualize the "group" in technologically mediated contexts. Although we agree with Lichtman (2011) about the need for further research on the nature, affordances, and functions of online focus group work, we also think that much conceptual work needs to be done with respect to units of analysis that motivate such research, differences in the specific constitutions of different interactional/communicative modalities, and our understandings of private, public, and the relations between the two.

Conclusions

The future of focus group research is wide open. New uses and affordances will certainly emerge as new conceptual breakthroughs are made with respect to qualitative inquiry generally, as researchers explore and exploit their affordances, and as new tools and environments for conducting research proliferate. It is, of course, impossible even to imagine future intersections between social media and focus group methodology. If history is any guide, our predictions would probably overstate the impact of these possible intersections in the short term and understate them in the long term. As focus groups are increasingly "opened up" in new ways, their mediation across time and place will create a host of new possibilities for research. As Stewart and Williams (2007) argued,

> the advent of Internet and networked communications has resulted in the proliferation of new social spaces, devoid of physicality. Adapted and adaptive social science research methods more generally allow for the collection and analysis of data from these diverse populations. These reengineered method-ologies and methods can take advantage of these social worlds.
>
> (p. 413)

We would add here that our methods and methodologies have yet to catch up with the new and emergent social spaces to which Stewart and Williams refer. Indeed, there is a great deal of conceptual and methodological work we need to do to develop tools that will allow us to explore and understand these worlds and their potentials fully.

Conducting focus group work in virtual worlds also raises new questions and re-inflects old ones. Take the question of anonymity, for instance. The disem-bodied nature of social media allows participants to take on new roles and identities. This could help participants engage more openly and honestly when discussing potentially embarrassing or sensitive topics. It could also allow participants to speak more freely and honestly than they would in face-to-face settings. Yet, the reverse could be true as well. The disembodied nature of social media could allow participants to act in ways unconstrained by social conventions. Increased anonymity could also allow people to deceive others about their identities in ways that matter—both for the well being of others and for the research. How might talk and social interaction unfold, for example, in a study of racial differences in a social media context, if participants' racial backgrounds were only known through self-report? And how would we make sense of data gathered in such a study?

Anonymity is only one of the many issues we need to (re)consider as new information technologies proliferate. The issue of "community" is another. The disembodied nature of social media allows participants to create new forms of community—affinity groups, clusters, and spokescouncils, for example. These and other new social formation types make it very clear that social space itself is being re-imagined and reconstituted in new ways. Participants from across the globe can now communicate with each other instantly, in real time. They can initiate and deploy social movement agendas in rhizomatic fashion. Yet, whether and how the interactional dynamics (and effects) possible in virtual environments will be the same or different from those in proximal interactions remains almost completely unknown. The "proliferation of new social spaces" brings with it enormous potentials and possibilities for all of the functions of focus group work we discussed in the book (inquiry, pedagogy, and politics). But it ushers in new questions, concerns, and even dangers as well. How important, for example, is embodied, face-to-face presence in the creation of community? Can community itself be mediated? Will the glue that binds community in virtual landscapes be weaker or stronger than the glue that binds community in more traditional social landscapes? As Sherry Turkle and others have made clear, mediated communication often has a striated or formatted feel to it. "The simple clarities of our globalized computer worlds depend on their virtuality. The real world is messy and painted in shades of grey. In that world we need to be comfortable with ambivalence and contradiction" (Turkle, 2004, p. 112). Do social media environments reduce complexity and contradiction thus affording only more superficial connections between and among people? If so, what might be the consequences for research of conducting focus groups in these environments?

These questions all have ethical implications as well, some of which we have already broached (e.g. protecting anonymity and detecting deception). Other implications with respect to other issues such as privacy, trust, transparency, control of content, and public welfare are relevant here as well and will need to be addressed. As we have suggested throughout, however, practical ethical problems index even more crucial conceptual ones. Current research ethics policies and practices are predicated on the fully rational autonomous self of the Enlightenment. This conception of "self"—and Enlightenment thinking generally—has tended to reinforce a sharp split between public and private domains. Considering ethical questions with the collective (rather than the individual) at the center of things provides another angle of vision on these questions. And when the idea of the collective (or community) itself is troubled and expended within social media landscapes, more new angles of vision are likely to emerge. If, as we have suggested, focus group research has already challenged the Enlightenment self and the public-private split, then focus group research in virtual worlds is likely to challenge them even more. What are the possible forms that research ethics might take in such worlds? Might these worlds help us imagine more social, communal, and democratic forms of ethics?

These issues (and many similar ones) are indeed pressing. One can read the so-called Arab Spring and the Occupy Wall Street movements through them. On the one hand, these and other worldwide protests and revolutions were enabled by social media like Facebook. New forms of community were imagined and created. Private concerns became public. Regimes fell and new concerns around inequality came to the fore. On the other hand, lasting political movements and interventions depend upon deep and abiding social connections and ties. The fates of these new forms of community are indeed unknown. Will they last? If so, what will account for their stability? Will they transmogrify? If so, how? And what will account for their shape shifting? These are very much open questions, the answers to which have important consequences for focus group research in the future. Suffice it to say that with the world changing as fast as it is, imagining how the forms, functions, and affordances of focus groups and focus group work might change in the wake of this changing world is dizzying indeed. Would that we had a crystal ball.

Epilogue

We would now like to offer some final thoughts about this book. In Chapters 1 and 2 we discussed the history of focus group work. Much of this work evolved in applied contexts—marketing, advertising, propaganda studies, health sciences, and so on. Typically, the goal of focus group work in these contexts was to gauge the effects of prescribed and delimited messages, products, and practices. Recall that "focus" was the methodological breakthrough in the earliest focus group work—a move that allowed for a particular kind of "scaling up" that often ignored the role of the "group." Whereas most other books and treatises on focus groups have attempted to think through the nature of focus groups or to outline procedures for conducting them, we have attempted a more systematic historical and conceptual interrogation of the nature, functions, and affordances of focus group work in relation to contemporary debates about inquiry and method.

In this regard, the organization of the book has been intentional and strategic. The three primary functions of focus group work emerged through a systematic historical investigation of the use of focus groups since the pioneering studies of Robert Merton and his colleagues. The quasi-unique affordances of focus group work emerged in and through the discovery/production of these functions and seem constitutively related to them. And our recommended practices were developed in relation to exploring and exploiting these affordances.

Although we did not intend this book to be a "how to" book—a point we are sure is evident by now—we do think it is practical in many ways. Our extended arguments about the importance of thinking about theory, history, and method simultaneously have important implications for actual research practice. Because we have seen questions of method reduced to questions of technique alone all too often, we have tried to provide an antidote to this tendency. We have done this by arguing that techniques are always developed from within particular episte- mological worldviews and conceptual frameworks and that their complex histories of use produce multiple affordances. An informed, principled use of research strategies and methods thus requires in-depth understanding of the co-evolution of theoretical, historical, and practical dimensions of any technique or strategy one might use—focus groups for example. Additionally, interrogating the con- ceptual foundations and histories of method allows one to interrogate our epistemologies and how these epistemologies inform how we understand the world.

We hope this book has provided some tools for doing this kind of intellectual work. We also hope the book can be used for practical purposes as well, but practical purposes enacted in sophisticated rather than simple ways. In this spirit, we end this book by posing some questions and offering some musings in relation to them. Both the questions and the musings are grounded on our arguments about how the affordances of focus group research have emerged from the functions of focus group research, which have emerged from the complex and variegated history of focus group research.

How does one begin to frame a research project? Novice researchers are often cautioned against letting "method" drive research topics and questions. In many ways, this is good advice, but it is not airtight. Given all that we have said about the histories, functions, and affordances of focus group work, it is worth revisiting the distinction between research object and method, as well as the question of whether developing research questions should always precede choosing research strategies. For some projects—ones that pivot on naturalistic, dynamic social interaction and where the collective is clearly the unit of analysis—a researcher may know that focus groups are essential to the project even before research questions are finalized. Indeed, this was the case with George's study, which was, in many ways, modeled after second- and third-wave feminist consciousness raising groups. It was also the case with Greg's study, which built upon and extended the practice of conducting dialogic literature discussions in English language arts classrooms in the United States (e.g. Applebee, 1996; Nystrand, 1997).

How will you puzzle through the ways research questions and research methods might play out in your own work? Where or to whom might you appeal for help in this process?

How does one choose a site for conducting focus group work? As we argued in Chapter 4, location matters, especially with respect to issues of safety, comfort, and community building. Focus groups can, of course, be held anywhere. One needs to decide whether the setting and the study are of a piece as was the case in Janice Radway's study of romance novel enthusiasts and Greg's study of young people's investments in popular culture. Even if setting and study are not of a piece, most studies cannot simply be conducted anywhere with the expectation of generating the same findings. Recall that, in George's study of new immigrant women, changing the venue of focus groups from the YWCA where participants took ESL classes to the participants' homes made a huge difference in how the women opened up, how community developed, and what data were produced. The common denominator here though is that holding focus groups in spaces that are familiar to, safe, and comfortable to participants is fundamentally important. As we tried to show through our examples, such spaces maximize the ways in which both the functions and the affordances of focus group work can be enacted.

What space or spaces do you think might work best for your focus group study? Why? How might these spaces help you make the most of the functions and affordances of focus group work?

Who will your participants be? There are many ways to answer this question. We have advocated for exploiting pre-existing networks because they tend to encourage collegiality and solidarity building. In most of the studies we discussed, including our own, groups were homogeneous. However, for some research projects, strategically assembling people with different interests, perspectives, and motives might make more sense. Recall that we wondered whether and how more heterogeneous groups in Greg's study of adolescents' investment in popular culture might have resulted in different amounts and kinds of data. Recall also that we wondered how focus group conversations about gendered relationships would have gone if both men and women were involved. Doubtless things would have gone differently in both cases. We just don't know how. However, Michelle Fine and her colleagues in the Echoes Project chose to assemble groups composed of young people who did not normally interact with each other—people from across the ethnic, economic, and racial spectrum. Their hunches paid off in the sense that very dynamic, contested conversations occurred in their focus groups. Additionally, these groups produced very rich data, especially with respect to how participants understood the perspectives of others very different from themselves, interacted with those others, dealt with apparent contradictions, negotiated differences when they arose, and resolved conflicts.

Who will you recruit to be in your focus groups? Why? What advantages and disadvantages do you see in having more homogeneous versus more heterogeneous groups? Why?

How will you recruit your participants? Again, there are many ways to answer this question. In Janice Radway's study, she enlisted the help of Dot, the bookstore owner whom the women she wanted to recruit knew, admired, and trusted. Greg's participants were, in a way, "found art"—friendship cliques at the community center where he conducted his study. He realized that friendship cliques would make great focus group participants almost as soon as he began to understand the *ethos* and *worldview* of the community center and the community it served. The same was true for Mitchell Duenier and his *Slim's Table* study. George began his recruitment process by posting flyers on bulletin boards in buildings where his desired participants took classes, worked, gathered, and worshipped. This strategy was modestly successful at best. It did, however, produce a couple of participants who were really interested in the study and who helped George recruit a dynamic, stable group of participants exploiting their friendship networks. As you can see, sometimes these decisions can be made strategically and in advance. Sometimes it is better to wait until you have fairly well-developed understandings of the ethos and worldview of the collectives you want to study and the site(s) where you will conduct your research. Sometimes what seem to be principled, sensible recruitment plans do not pan out, and you need to develop new ones.

What kinds of recruitment strategies do you think might be most effective for your project? Why? What problems or issues or do you think you might encounter in recruiting participants. How might you work through these problems?

What about facilitation strategies? As indexed in the book's title and as we noted in Chapter 1, focus groups range from structured interviews to the collective conversations. Facilitators operate on a continuum from more active and directive to more participatory to more passive and non-directive. We are sure that our biases have shown through with regard to this issue. We think that a more "hands off" approach to facilitation results in drawing out the unique and powerful functions and affordances of focus groups more fully.

In this regard, we have advocated using maximally open-ended prompts, letting participants take over the flow of talk and social interaction, encouraging solidarity building, and eventually becoming dispensable because the groups have become self-sufficient. Some researchers, especially novice ones, find this non-autocratic approach uncomfortable and difficult to maintain. Our suggestion for these researchers would be to ease into a more non-directive approach to facilitation slowly and deliberately, paying close attention to the effects of different ways of facilitating participants' activity.

We have also advocated keeping notes, following up on key themes and gaps, listening for *breakdowns* and *subtexts*, and asking for elaboration on issues that remain. One could, of course, choose to be more focused and directive from the outset, though this would likely constrain the range of participants' responses. Having admitted our biases, and having made these recommendations, we also realize that a more directive approach may work better in some projects and contexts. Exactly how to facilitate focus groups and whether and when to change one's facilitation style are questions that require considerable reflection and can only be answered in the thick of things and often in collaboration with fellow researchers and research participants.

So, on the continuum from structured interviews to collective conversations, where do you think you should position yourself for your project? Why? What changes do you anticipate making as your research unfolds? Why do you suppose these changes will enhance the research process?

When is it time to end a focus group study? This is a difficult question to answer and often depends upon a host of factors from funding to time availability (both of researchers and research participants) to impasses in the process of discovery to data saturation to disruption by unexpected and even traumatic events, just to name a few. Additionally, ending almost any study—but especially a focus group study because of the relationships that are forged from doing this kind of work—is usually a complicated and difficult process. Under normal circumstances (i.e. no traumatic reasons for ending), the standard and still helpful response is to end a study when one reaches data saturation. That is, one ends when one begins to hear the same responses again and again. However, there are a variety of reasons why one might want to continue a study or to introduce a new angle on the study

References

Anderson, N. (1923). *The Hobo*. Chicago: University of Chicago Press.

Ang, I. (1985). *Watching Dallas*. London: Routledge.

Appadurai, A. (1990). Disjuncture and difference in the global cultural economy. *Public Culture*, *2*(2), 1–24.

Applebee, A. (1996). *Curriculum as Conversation: Transforming Traditions of Teaching and Learning*. Chicago: University of Chicago Press.

Bakhtin, M. M. (1990). *Art and Answerability: Early Philosophical Essays by M. M. Bakhtin* (V. Liapunov, Trans.; M. Holquist and V. Liapunov, eds.). Austin, TX: University of Texas Press.

Bakhtin, M. M. (1993). *Toward a Philosophy of the Act* (V. Liapunov, Trans.; V. Liapunov and M. Holquist, eds). Austin, TX: University of Texas Press.

Barbour, R. (2008) *Defining Focus Groups*. Thousand Oaks, CA: Sage.

Barbour, R., and Kitzinger, J. (1999). *Developing Focus Group Research*. Thousand Oaks, CA: Sage.

Behar, R. (1993). *Translated Woman: Crossing the Border with Esperanza's Story*. Boston: Beacon.

Berger, P., and Luckmann, T. (1966). *The Social Construction of Reality*. New York: Doubleday.

Bishop, R., Berryman, M., Cavanagh, T., Teddy, L., and Clapham, S. (2006). *Te Kotahitanga Phase 3 Whakawhanaungatanga: Establishing a Culturally Responsive Pedagogy of Relations in Mainstream Secondary School Classrooms*. Wellington, NZ: Ministry of Education.

Bloor, M., Frankland, J., Thomas, M., and Robson, K. (2001). *Focus Groups in Social Research*. Thousand Oaks, CA: Sage.

Bourdieu, P. (1990). *The Logic of Practice*. Cambridge: Cambridge University Press.

Briller, S., Schim, S. M., Meert, K. L., and Thurston, C. S. (2007/2008). Special considerations bereavement focus groups. *Omega: Journal of Death and Dying*, *56*(3), 255–271.

Brüggen, E., and Willems, P. (2009). A critical comparison of offline focus groups, online focus groups and e-Delphi. *International Journal of Market Research*, *51*(3), 363–381.

Cammarota, J., and Fine, M. (eds) (2008). *Revolutionizing Education*. New York: Routledge.

Christians, C. (2011). Ethics and politics in qualitative research. In N. Denzin and Y. Lincoln (eds), *The Handbook of Qualitative Research* (pp. 61–80). Thousand Oaks, CA: Sage.

CNN (2008) CNN pulls out all stops for coverage of first McCain-Obama presidential debate. Available at www.gwu.edu/~action/2008/chrndeb08/cnn092308pr.html, accessed on July 25, 2012.

CNN Transcripts (2008). Anderson Cooper 360 Degrees: Analysis of the Second Presidential Debates. Available at http://transcripts.cnn.com/TRANSCRIPTS/0810/07/acd.02.html, accessed on August 2, 2012.

Cooper, T. J., Baturo, A. R., Duus, E. A., and Moore, K. M. (2008). Indigenous vocational students, culturally effective communities of practice and mathematics understanding. In O. Figueras, J. L. Cortina, S. Alatorre, T. Rojano, and A. Sepulveda (eds), *Proceedings of the 32nd Annual Conference of the International Group for the Psychology of Mathematics Education* (pp. 378–384). Morelia, Mexico: PME.

Creswell, J. W. (2002) *Qualitative, Quantitative, and Mixed-Methods Approaches* (Revised ed.). Thousand Oaks, CA: Sage.

deCerteau, M. (1984). *The Practice of Everyday Life* (S. F. Rendall, Trans.). Berkeley, CA: University of California Press.

Deleuze, G., and Guattari, F. (1987). *A Thousand Plateaus: Capitalism & Schizophrenia* (B. Massumi, Trans.). Minneapolis: University of Minnesota Press.

Denzin, N. K., and Lincoln, Y. S. (2005). Epilogue: The eighth and ninth moments—qualitative research in/and the fractures future. In N. K. Denzin and Y. S. Lincoln (eds), *The Sage Handbook of Qualitative Research* (3rd ed.) (pp. 1115–1126). Thousand Oaks, CA: Sage.

Denzin, N. K., and Lincoln, Y. S. (2011). Epilogue: Toward a "refunctioned ethnography." In N. K. Denzin and Y. S. Lincoln (eds), *The Sage Handbook of Qualitative Research* (4th ed.) (pp. 715–718). Thousand Oaks, CA: Sage.

Dill, B. T. (1994). Fictive kin, paper sons, and compadrazgo: Women of color and the struggle for family survival. In M. B. Zinn and B. T. Dill (eds), *Women of Color in U.S. Society* (pp. 149–169). Philadelphia: Temple University Press.

Dimitriadis, G. (2001). *Performing Identity/Performing Culture: Hip Hop as Text, Pedagogy and Lived Practice.* New York: Peter Lang.

Duneier, M. (1994). *Slim's Table: Race, Respectability, and Masculinity.* Chicago: University of Chicago Press.

Eisenstein, H. (1984). *Contemporary Feminist Thought.* New York: Macmillan.

Erickson, F. (2004). *Talk and Social Theory.* London: Polity.

Espiritu, Y. L. (1997). *Asian Women and Men: Labor, Laws, and Love.* Thousand Oaks, CA: Sage.

Fairclough, N. (1995). *Media Discourse.* London: Edward Arnold.

Fetene, G. (2009). Self-reported sexual experiences, sexual conduct and safer sex practices of Ethiopian undergraduate male and female students in the context of the HIV/AIDS pandemic (doctoral dissertation). University at Buffalo, State University of New York.

Fetene, G., and Dimitriadis, G. (2010). Globalization, public policy, and the 'knowledge gap.' *Journal of Education Policy, 25*(4), 425–441.

Fine, M. (2006). Bearing witness: Methods for researching oppression and resistance. *Social Justice Research, 19*(1), 83–108.

Fine, M. and Weis, L. (1998). *The Unknown City.* Boston: Beacon Press.

Foucault, M. (1979). *Discipline and Punish: The Birth of the Prison* (A. Sheridan, Trans.). New York: Vintage Books.

Foucault, M. (1984). Nietzsche, genealogy, and history. In P. Rabinow (ed.), *The Foucault Reader* (pp. 76–100). New York: Pantheon Books.

Fox, F., Morris, M., and Rumsey, N. (2007). Doing synchronous online focus groups with young people. *Qualitative Health Research, 17*(4), 529–538.

Freire, P. (1993/1970). *Pedagogy of the Oppressed.* New York: Continuum.

Gee, J. P. (2011). *Social Linguistics and Literacies: Ideologies in Discourse.* New York: Routledge.

Gere, A. R. (1987). *Writing Groups: History, Theory, and Implications.* Carbondale, IL: Southern Illinois University Press.

Gergen, K., and Gergen, M. (2012). *Playing with Purpose*. Walnut Creek, CA: Left Coast Press.

Gilkes, C. T. (1994). "If it wasn't for the women. . .": African American women, community work, and social change. In M. B. Zinn and B. T. Dill (eds), *Women of Color in U.S. Society* (pp. 229–246). Philadelphia: Temple University Press.

Grand, S. (2004). *Red Pedagogy: Native America Social and Political Thought*. Lanham, MD: Rowman & Littlefield.

Gutmann, A. and Thompson, T. (1996). *Democracy and Disagreement*. Cambridge, MA: Harvard University Press.

Hall, K., Williams, L., and Daniel, L. (2010). An afterschool program for economically disadvantaged youth: Perceptions of parents, staff, and students. *Research in the Schools*, *17*(1), 12–28.

Happell, B. (2007). Focus groups in nursing research: an appropriate method or the latest fad? *Nurse Researcher*, *14*(2), 18–24.

Heidegger, M. (1962/1927). *Being and Time* (J. Macquarrie and E. Robinson, Trans.). Oxford: Blackwell.

Heidegger, M. (1971). *Poetry, Language, Thought* (A. Hofstadter, Trans.). New York: Harper & Row.

Heidegger, M. (1993). What is metaphysics? In D. F. Krell (ed.) *Martin Heidegger: Basic Writings*, Revised and Expanded Edition (pp. 93–110). London: Routledge.

Hesse-Biber, S., and Leavy, P. (eds). (2006). *Handbook of Emergent Methods*. Thousand Oaks, CA: Sage.

Hill, M. L. (2009). *Beats, Rhymes, and Classroom Life*. New York: Teachers College Press.

hooks, b. (1989). *Talking Back: Thinking Feminist, Thinking Black*. Cambridge, MA: South End Press.

Hopson, L., and Steiker, L. (2008). Methodology for evaluating an adaption of evidence-based drug abuse prevention in alternative schools. *Children & Schools*, *30*(2), 116–127.

Kamberelis, G., and Dimitriadis, G. (2005). *On Qualitative Inquiry: Approaches to Language and Literacy Research*. New York: Teachers College Press.

Kotler, P., and Zaltman, G. (1971). Social marketing: An approach to planned social change. *The Journal of Marketing*, *35*(3), 3–12.

Kreisler, H. (2002). Activism, anarchism, and power: Conversation with Noam Chomsky, linguist and political activist. University of California at Berkeley, Institute of International Studies, Conversation with History Series. Available at http://globetrotter.berkeley.edu/people2/Chomsky/chomsky-con0.html, accessed August 1, 2009.

Kress, V., and Shoffner, M. (2007). Focus groups: A practical and applied research approach for counselors. *Journal of Counseling and Development*, *85*, 189–196.

Kreuger, R. A. and Casey, M. A. (2008) *Focus Groups: A Practical Guide for Applied Research*. Thousand Oaks, CA: Sage.

Lather, P. (2001). Postbook: Working the ruins of feminist ethnography. *Signs: Journal of Women in Culture and Society*, *27*(1), 199–227.

Lather, P. (2007). *Getting Lost: Feminist Efforts Toward a Double(d) Science*. Albany, NY: State University of New York Press.

Lather, P., and Smithies, C. (1997). *Troubling the Angels: Women Living with HIV/AIDS*. Boulder, CO: Westview Press.

Lee, R. (2010). The secret life of focus groups: Robert Merton and the diffusion of a research method. *American Sociology*, *41*, 115–141.

Levine, P. (2008). A public voice for youth. In L. Bennett (ed.), *Civic Voice Online*. Washington DC: The John and Catherine Macarthur Foundation.

Lichtman, M. (2011). *Qualitative Research in Education*. Thousand Oaks, CA: Sage.

Liebes, T., and Katz, E. (1990). *The Export of Meaning: Cross-cultural Readings of Dallas*. Oxford: Oxford University Press.

Madison, D., and Hamera, J. (2006). Introduction. In D. Madison and J. Hamera (eds), *Handbook of Performance Studies*. Thousand Oaks, CA: Sage.

Madriz, E. (2000). Focus groups in feminist research. In N. K. Denzin and Y. S. Lincoln (eds), *Handbook of Qualitative Research* (2nd ed.) (pp. 835–850). Thousand Oaks, CA: Sage.

Madriz, E. (1997). *Nothing Bad Happens to Good Girls: Fear of Crime in Women's Lives*. Berkeley, CA: University of California Press.

Marcus, G. E. (1998). *Ethnography Through Thick and Thin*. Princeton, NJ: Princeton University Press.

Martin, E. (1995). *Flexible Bodies: Tracking Immunity in American Culture—From the Days of Polio to the Age of AIDS*. Boston: Beacon Press.

Merton, R., and Kendall, P. (1946). The focused interview. *The American Journal of Sociology, 51*(6), 541–557.

Merton, R. (1987). The focused group interview and focus groups: Continuities and discontinuities. *Public Opinion Quarterly, 51*, 550–566.

Merton, R. (1990). *The Focused Interview* (2nd ed.). New York: Free Press.

Ministry of Health, Disease Prevention and Control Department (2004). *AIDS in Ethiopia: Fifth Report*. Addis Ababa: Ministry of Health.

Morley, D. (1980). *The "Nationwide" Audience*. London: British Film Institute.

Nabors, L., Ramos, V., and Weist, M. D. (2001). Use of focus groups as a tool for evaluating programs for children and families. *Journal of Education & Psychological Consultation, 12*(3), 243–256.

Nelson-Gardell, D. (2001). The voices of victims: Surviving child abuse. *Child & Adolescent Social Work Journal, 18*(6), 401–416.

Nystrand, M. (1997). *Opening Dialogue: Understanding the Dynamics of Language and Learning in the English Classroom*. New York: Teachers College Press.

Parahoo, K. (2007). Focus groups. *Nurse Researcher, 14*(2), 4–6.

Peters, R. (2009). Using focus groups and stakeholders to revise the MPA curriculum. *Journal of Public Affairs Education, 15*(1), 1–16.

Radway, J. (1984). *Reading the Romance: Women, Patriarchy, and Popular Literature*. Durham, NC: University of North Carolina Press.

Richardson, L. (2000). Writing: A method of inquiry. In N. Denzin and Y. Lincoln (eds), *Handbook of Qualitative Research* (2nd ed.) (pp. 923–948). Thousand Oaks, CA: Sage.

Schearer, S. B. (1981) The value of focus group research for social action programs. *Studies in Family Planning, 12*, 407–408.

Smith, P. (1988). *Discerning the Subject*. Minneapolis: University of Minnesota Press.

Stewart, K., and Williams, M. (2007). Researching online populations: The use of online focus groups for social research. *Qualitative Research, 5*(4), 395–416.

Teddlie, C. B., and Tashakkori, A. (2008). *Foundations of Mixed Methods Research: Integrating Quantitative and Qualitative Approaches in the Social and Behavioral Sciences*. Thousand Oaks, CA: Sage.

Thrasher, F. (1927). *The Gang*. Chicago: University of Chicago Press.

Tipping, J. (1998). Focus groups: A method of needs assessment. *Journal of Continuing Education in the Health Professions, 18*(3), 150–154.

Torre, M., and Fine, M. (2006). Researching and resisting. In S. Ginwright, P. Nogurea, and J. Cammarota (eds), *Beyond Resistance* (pp. 269–283). New York: Routledge.

Torre, M., and Fine, M., with Alexander, N., Billups, A. B., Blanding, Y., Genao, E., Marboe, E., Salah, T., and Urdang, K. (2008). PAR in the contact zone. In J. Cammarota and M. Fine (eds), *Revolutionizing Education* (pp. 23–44). New York: Routledge.

Tuck. E. (2008). Gate-ways and Get-Aways (doctoral dissertation). CUNY Graduate Center.

Tuck, E. (2012). *Urban Youth and School Pushout: Gateways, Get-Aways, and the GED.* New York: Routledge.

Tuckel, P. and Wood, M. (2001). Respondent cooperation in focus groups. *International Journal of Market Research*, 43(4), 391–408.

Turkle, S. (2004). The fellowship of the microchip. In M. Suarez-Orozco and D. Qin-Hillard (eds), *Globalization: Education and Culture in the New Millennium* (pp. 97–112). Berkeley, CA: University of California Press.

Turner, V. (1969). *The Ritual Process: Structure and Anti-Structure.* New York: Aldine.

Weis, L. (2004). Race, gender, and critique. In L. Weis and M. Fine (eds), *Working Methods* (pp. 27–51). New York: Routledge.

Wertsch, J. V. (2002). *Voices of Collective Remembering.* Cambridge, UK: Cambridge University Press.

Whyte, W. F. (1993/1943). *Street Corner Society.* Chicago: University of Chicago Press.

Wilson, W. A., and Yellow Bird, M. (2005). *For Indigenous Eyes Only: A Decolonization Handbook.* Santa Fe, NM: School of American Research Press.

Wirth, L. (1928). *The Ghetto.* Chicago: University of Chicago Press.

Wyatt, T., Krauskopf, P., and Davidson, R. (2008). Using focus groups for program planning and evaluation. *Journal of School Nursing*, 24(2), 71–77.

York, V., Brannon, L., Roberts, K., Shanklin, C., and Howells, A. (2009). Using the theory of planned behavior to elicit restaurant employee beliefs about food safety. *Journal of Foodservice Business Research*, 12(2), 180–197.

Index